1

The World Wide Web of Wonderful Men

The shirtless Erik Estrada lookalike who refused to believe that he is not God's gift to any and every woman, the grifter who almost tricked me into buying him a used Corvette, a widowed "professor" wearing a dead squirrel on his head, local lads of all ages and men from as far away as New Zealand, a cruel Scotsman calling in the middle of the night, a sweet Phil Collins twin, a salesman too good to look for love online – just ask him, a guy disappointed that I didn't look just like Suzanne Somers (thirty years ago) describing his wife as "large" and spending all her time reading romance novels, many "nice" men single after their wives checked out of the marriage, sad widowers, a 50 something man still in love with a girl he hasn't seen since second grade and the ghost of whom destroyed his marriage, men who claim to own boats and men who want to be treated to all expenses paid cruises, a great guy in Cincinnati, a London cop, men who will "allow" their new wives to work part-time and men horribly in debt, and the year younger than my son suitor who wanted to move in with me. He'll break up with his current girlfriend – it's my choice.

After several years of actively pursuing love and romance online, I'm still single. Single, as in sitting at home on this particular Saturday night, coloring my hair, giving myself a facial and relaxing. I'm not in front of a computer screen being bombarded by IMs and furiously answering emails, or waiting for someone to call.

Now that I'm less interested (less desperate), my inbox is filled with responses from men to today's request for a platonic movie date.

Nice guys (and unfortunately, they do seem to finish last) are everywhere along with a few less reputable characters.

What is scarce in the Worldwide Web of Wonderful Men is chemistry. Who wants to be like cousin Alice's dog Daisy who didn't need to be spayed because no male dog ever came calling even when she was in heat? There was strong chemistry between the much too much younger suitor and me, but is it wise to base a relationship solely on a case of the wants? Is it possible to have a relationship without strong attraction? How on earth can a couple survive without chemistry?

Being willing to relocate is a deal-breaker, and if you're

willing, you quite possibly could be married shortly after posting a profile.

Gandulf wanted an American bride because he feels we hold our looks longer than the *fraus* he knows. A German engineer = good provider.   My tap root is a foot deep, so I'm not going anywhere, but this man was perfect for a more flexible woman. (I'd never once considered that I could be inflexible, so this took me by surprise.)

Oh! By Internet dating, you will learn about yourself: your likes, dislikes, temperament. All these years I thought I was an adventurous soul, ready to take off on a moment's notice, and although that is true to an extent, there are things I absolutely will not even consider.

What are your "never will – don't even ask me" boundaries? Do you insist on having an indoor pet or not having any? Will you move? Change careers? Have children? Raise someone else's children/grandchildren?   Refuse to take up bass fishing? Spend your week-ends watching a man watch tv? Even worse – watch your new guy sit and drink his life away? Become active in his church? Become a recluse? Have liposuction?   Cut your hair? Grow your hair?

I would convert to another denomination of my own religion, learn to cook all his favorite foods, attempt to keep house, continue to be practical and low maintenance, work full-time, not overspend – well, not much, wear beautiful lingerie, be his biggest cheerleader, love him forever, be kind, loving and affectionate, and share his interests. However, my two little darling dogs that family and friends consider annoying at best are part of a package deal. I will not relocate. Being widowed relatively young created an insecurity that will force me to always work full-time so being someone's traveling buddy is out of the question. Yes, yes, I could be missing out on a lifestyle that most women can only dream about. I also could be strolling through life with my eyes wide open.

I began Internet dating with anticipation. The men! So many! Attentive men!! I made mistakes, several serious (believing all the bull being slung and never quite understanding that, no, a man is not flying from England to meet me) and one fatal (posting a picture of myself when I was twenty pounds thinner – MISTAKE ONE -- which I admitted), that I'll share with you later.

I've refused several men who have asked me to meet them for coffee. Why? Do you ever think that any man that cheap with his money would also be cheap with his emotions? One guy told me he was tired of paying for dates. If a woman isn't worth half a pizza or coffee plus dessert, how important or interesting can she be?

So, as you have figured out, it's not as easy as the tv ads make it seem. One problem that falls solely on my shoulders is that only The Thunderbolt will satisfy my romantic nature. Love at first sight does exist because it has happened to me twice: in one instance it lasted until death did us part and the other was impossible due to his prior commitment. Both occurred in real life, and the stars did collide.

The best Internet date? He drove a truckload of firewood in a snowstorm from Cincinnati, bought my grown daughter a winter coat, and took me to dinner. He was tall and well built and above all, nice – and "normal." However, he was also a hopeless romantic and was disappointed when we didn't immediately fall into each other's arms. I would have, and probably should have, but there was a shadow standing between us. The good? Born four days after my husband, he seemed just like him. The bad? Born four days after my husband, he seemed just like him. An example, you ask? I was married to a man who spent an inordinate amount of time thinking and talking about groundhogs. He hated them. Fake Bill? He called me one night and talked about ... groundhogs. The difference? He thought they were cute.

Since you are reading this, you probably have some interest in giving the Internet a try. Have fun, but keep your powder dry. We don't want broken hearts.

2

True Confessions

In my years of Internet dating, I've met them all, characters and charmers, most of them very nice men. However, I am holding out for The Thunderbolt to strike me, as it has in the past, in real life, twice. The first time Lightening hit, I was twenty, and we were together for thirty years, through good and bad, parents of two, until death did us part. Like many long term relationships, it had its ups and downs, and toward the end, it was unfortunately more downs than ups. Still, or perhaps because of the downs, his death devastated me. Afraid of life, lonely and living alone for the first time, suddenly totally responsible for my life, I set a goal to be remarried within a year. MISTAKE TWO.

Not wanting to waste time, I met many guys, quickly. While it did weed out the mismatches, it also highlighted the fact that almost no man and I clicked. Knowing that most men didn't want me, even ones I wasn't interested in, dinged my confidence. Was I too fat? For those into the anorexic, definitely. Was my grooming less than impeccable? That's a good possibility, as I take are of animals and garden. Was I too unassuming? Yes, that is also a definite. Since I don't like braggarts and people I know who refer to themselves as "assertive" come across to me as aggressive, no-nonsense, straight arrow borefests, I deliberately downplay my assets.

Perhaps you can learn from my mistakes, or maybe you will be entertained by my often misguided search for love.

I recently went on my last date. Oh! Are you thinking I met the love of my life and we are going to live happily ever after and that's is why I am no longer dating? Sorry to disillusion you, but after trying dating site after dating site and the pickin's being slim, I found the quality of the men I was meeting actually getting worse as time went on. So – meeting men by chance in real life, bring it on, baby! Let's call a truce and take a time out.

This is not meant to be judgmental, and perhaps the men and I just were not compatible. As in: I work two jobs and he is unemployed and living with (and off) his 83 year old parents, just until some kind of disability kicks in. There's nothing physically wrong with him, but when he lost his manufacturing job he found it impossible to replace it. And you can't expect him to work at a job that pays not much more than minimum wage, can you? And the fact that his lawyer hasn't been able to get him disability doesn't mean he should give up, does it? Besides, his parents are glad he moved back in with them.

After going on date after date, am I disappointed? Of course! I'd love to meet the love of my life! But through my journey I learned that "love" depends on chemistry. And chemistry cannot come through a computer monitor.

While men I met online were rejecting me as being in the league of the Mythical 300 Pound Woman (more about that later), younger, more attractive guys in real time were leaving notes on my car ("I think you are cute! Please call!") and asking their co-workers to tell me they wanted to date me. I did call the guy who left the note on my windshield, and I did meet him. I'm a walker, and he's a runner. When he told me that he came to Ohio on an athletic scholarship in 1994, I responded, "Uuhh. My son started college in 1994." He didn't care! Although I bought a silky pink blouse for a date, plans changed. But thank you! You are a sweetheart! And in that young guy's opinion, I was not fat, I was not old. I later dated another 28 year old, Fake Dead Guy, for a short time. Details of that "relationship" is sprinkled throughout this book.

The message of this book is, to paraphrase an old song, "you can't force love." The media bombards us with "happy endings" as well as frightening stories. Neither has happened to me. Love is just around the corner, I believe, but for the stars to collide, I need to stop hiding behind and depending upon a computer to fix my life and get out into the Real World!

While on hiatus, I still peruse the personals, but also have joined a hiking club, participated in metropolitan parks events, and writing a blog about my escapades exploring southern Ohio, northern West Virginia and Kentucky. No, I haven't met "him" but I've had fun.

If you have met Mr. Right or even Mr. Right Now via the web, congrats! Two close friends met their men through dating websites. After manys misfires and absolute disasters, one is married and mother of a toddler; the other, happily cohabitating.

A gay friend has started dating, as in building a relationship, a guy he met online. He, too, had more than his share of romantic disappointments, yet he continued his quest.

My daughter - *fingers crossed* - has met most of her boyfriends in Real Time, but posts a profile during Guy Droughts. Her first experience in the virtual arena was with a guy described as a Brady Brother, Twenty-first Century (Greg?). He borrowed his mom's car and drove twelve hours to meet her. She spent an entire day, nervously awaiting his arrival, then drove him from his motel room in Columbus to a restaurant near our home.

"You wear too much make-up." She never leaves the house without artfully applied war paint, but it's not "too much."

"You don't look anything like your picture." She looks exactly like her pictures and she posts recent ones.

"You are desperate…" She didn't respond to any of his criticisms but you can imagine her thoughts: I am not the one who drove twelve hours each way.

She drove him back to his motel room and let him out. She even brought her car to a full stop.

An older, wiser family friend said, "He would have walked the thirty miles back if it would have been me." Beverly has played the dating game for years, but she felt she hit the jackpot when she met her most memorable romantic partner, a man with an advanced degree who loved cats. She was thrilled when he gave her a Garfield mug. Yes, it had a chip in it, but she didn't care. Yes, it was a yard sale find with the price tag (five cents) still on it, but again, she liked him. When he decided he couldn't part with this valuable treasure and took it back, it mattered. He was cheap and stingy with everything, including his emotions.

She met him in Real Time. He probably was too cheap to have the Internet.

Where were we? Oh, yes. My daughter's new boyfriend, a dating site find, is single, attractive, ambitious, and they enjoy each other's company. And get this – they have no drama.

Along with my friends who are currently in relationships, my daughter's romantic good fortune has made me rethink cyber possibilities.

Did you love George Michael's *One More Try*? I think I hear it calling to me. It's time to post another profile.

There are advantages to giving Cupid a little electronic nudge. Internet dating is easier than cold calling, because unless you are at a bar, you never know who's available. Why waste your time flirting with someone who might be married, or otherwise involved, when with a few clicks of a mouse, you can find a man who is definitely out there looking for a good woman?

Getting back into the dating game is much easier with the Internet than it was for me starting out in my teens. When I complained to whom I then considered a friend that I couldn't get a date, meaning guys I liked never asked me out, not that I literally could not get any guy interested, her older sister gave my first name and phone number to a group of carnies who were in town a few days for our local fair. Eighteen year old seniors seemed so worldly to me, so you can imagine that as a sixteen year old virgin, very shy, I was terrified at the very idea of such independent, renegade men. Luckily, only one expressed interest, and my sternly religious mother scared him off. The older sister went on to pursue a checked career, and the "friend" is long out of my life.

There are sites for every taste and interest. A friend and I joined a dating service that matches animal lovers, but with our cat populations, we probably scared off men. Many of the people on this site appear to have one or two purebred pets, and my friend and I are rescuers (and some would say I at least am the one in need of rescuing). However, if you have one or two fancy dogs or cats, you would fit right in.

Another specialized site matches farmers with other farmers or people who would like to meet farmers. Relocating is not an option for me, so I didn't investigate, but if it were, this is the one site I would jump on! Farmers work long hours in isolated areas and don't have time to go out lookin' for love. They also are the ultimate family men. If you love the Great Outdoors, perhaps you could become Mrs. Mother Earth. You definitely would be appreciated. P.S. I knew if I joined, I would find a match, fall madly in love, and then try to figure out the logistics of holding on to my own place yet being with my plow boy.

Oh, Lord! I found a website that specializes in - my fantasy! - single firemen! The ones I see about town don't appear to need electronic help finding lady friends, but a local hero would be the answer to my prayers. Four alarm alert! This sounds Too Good to Be True. Join at your own risk.

There are also sites for people wanting to meet physicians. This is another group that we could presume would be beating away women with the proverbial stick, but if this is what you are looking for, it's there. Again, TGTBT.

Since one in four women has been exposed to genital herpes, there is a market for STD dating services. When meeting people from "normal" dating sites, when do you tell? Do you confide your deepest secret on a first date and risk losing the person forever? Do you wait until the eve of the first experience? Is that ethical? Are you old enough to remember when young women were advised to "confess" to a fiancé the night before the wedding that they had had premarital sex and/or given a child up for adoption? STD dating sites removes the worry about The Talk.

There are sites devoted to specific religions. The Catholic dating site I joined was at that time $6 a month, compared with an average of $25 for other sites.

Your completed profile will not only cover the basics such as height and weight, but also your favorite Bible verse (mine is the 23rd Psalm) and why (it leadeth me to still waters), and your favorite saint (Paul) and why (my son's name, which is also a family name).

After I signed up for the Catholic match, a very nice looking man contacted me. Never married, he had spent his adult life as a priest. Being widowed, not divorced, probably would have given me a few points. He was actively seeking a decent woman for a marriage similar to his parents (nine kids). He was from Boston, and I didn't want to move; he was very serious; and his desire for a large family could not include me as the mommy. Plain and simple: I'm too old. I said it, he didn't. He was attractive in every way, and had I been younger, it would have been worth the effort. Some woman was very lucky.

If you feel you need to lose a few pounds, check out any of the sites that cater to big beautiful people.

It might be important to you, but I never date (or search for dates) by age group. However, if you are interested in meeting a man of your generation, there are sites devoted to over 50, seniors, etc.

"Spoil" as in "I will spoil the right lady" and "lady wants to be spoiled" is one of the most common words in all of Internet Dating World. It is often capitalized. I don't want to be "Spoiled rotten" by anyone, and wonder about the sincerity of any man who makes this promise. Or perhaps he thinks having his woman standing in the middle of a field with a rope around her waist while he lifts a swimming pool liner is "spoiling" a woman. (This happened to me, but it was my husband, who I met in the "normal" way.)

Lady and its common misspelling, Ladie, is another commonly used word. Although I'm not much of a ladie or lady, and prefer to be called a woman, I do appreciate men being respectful.

Internet dating is still...dating. The same rules apply. Playing hard to get has worked for generations, and it isn't likely to change any time soon.

Don't contact a man first even if you think his profile is heavenly, don't inundate him with emails, don't send him links to things (in the name of friendship) that might interest him. Don't send him cute little cybercards "just because" any more than you would go out and buy them.

If a guy is interested in you, he will pursue you. If he isn't, he won't. Oh, there are shy guys, but usually they will get up the nerve, no matter what the cost to their egos, to contact you. That's where the fireworks come from!!

Curious, I checked out the ads of the competition.. The women in my age group looked nice and respectable, but there were no movie stars, and I felt better about myself. I really don't enjoy looking at pictures of women under thirty.

Also, when I began my Internet search, the 300 Pound Woman was very active in dating sites. (Perhaps men referred to me as such. Who knows? Who cares?)

Here are a few of the over thirty crowd: A full-figured country girl, late forties, likes taking care of a good man, looking for a relationship, not a one night stand. This is a person another woman would want for a friend, so I am guessing she will be snapped up by a decent guy.

One woman is in a wheelchair, but loves the outdoors. She's looking for a one-woman man, and no liars or cheaters need apply. According to conventional wisdom, never put anything negative in an ad. Keep things light and positive. Besides, is a liar going to admit he's a liar or a cheater that he takes on every woman in his sights?

Many women have a dog or cat, something that some men consider unwanted baggage. My pets are my babies, and although I don't ask a man to adore and adopt them, he has to accept that I'll always have at least one furry friend curled up on my bed.

One thing I am careful about is using capital letters to begin sentences, correct spelling and decent grammar. If I truly don't know how to spell a certain word, I go for a synonym! However, some of the best men can't spell, and I don't care! As I told one, I'm not your English teacher.

I did respond to a man who was looking for a "discreet" relationship, telling him since every other guy is looking for "discrete" he earns points for knowing the difference. However, I am not looking for a discreet relationship. Oh, baby, I want to meet Mr. Right and scream at the top of my lungs!

I do not visit men's webpages to view pictures and ongoing essays about their lives. We can email a few times, trade pictures, then talk on the phone and/or meet in person. Or he can move on. The same man (circa fifty years old) responded to both my ad and my daughter's with a link to his webpage. When I emailed him, he wrote back again suggesting I visit his webpage. Since I am looking for a real relationship, I didn't bother responding. If I want to read about someone and look at pictures, I'll go to celebrity websites. Jeff Gordon is much better looking than Mr. Visit My Page because I'm Too Lazy to Hold a Conversation with You.

❤ ►►

Amore – Fake Dead Guy Style!

For several months, I dated, very casually, a man half my age. Yes, you read that correctly. He is a year younger than my son, and I was no child bride. He's tall, blond, and cute. He has a brain or two. In other words, he didn't have to settle, and he apparently didn't feel that he did. We never were serious, so we never formally broke up. We are still friendly, and both still single. Although we live in the same town, population: 40,000, we did meet over the Internet, but not through a dating site. I met another serious suitor through the very same site and I can almost guarantee you would never be able to guess the type of site. Spoiler alert – findagrave! ❤

3

Deciphering Abbreviations and Commonly Used Terms

Before we get started, here are explanations for some common abbreviations and terms:

NSA = no strings attached. Run for the hills, sweetheart! This isn't false advertising. He really is going to do a hit and run on your heart, and other body parts.

ISO = in search of.

ROTFL = rolling on the floor laughing, not that anyone does.

LMAO or LMFAO = Laughing my [effing] ass off.

HWP = height, weight proportional. Many of us use a liberal interpretation to this phrase but we need to do an honest assessment of our bodies - otherwise, we are likely to get rejected. 5'2" and 180 pounds "evenly distributed" is not HWP. Also, "average" weight is not 250 pounds, even if you and your friends are in this range. Bending this requirement is the number one way to get humiliated, demeaned, rejected and otherwise insulted by a suitor. Take this from one who knows.

A few extra pounds. According to one honest to a fault guy, a few extra pounds are two or four and not a ounce more. Two to four extra pounds to most of us would equal HWP.

Good physical shape (according to one keyboard Romeo) = no hog-facing bags of White Castles while gulping and guzzling down liters of Dr. Pepper more than on the occasion of Halley's Comet passing through the sky. *Burp.*

HOH/DD = Head Of Household / Domestic Discipline. This appears to be spanking, but I'm not a child and I don't want a daddy, and even my daddy didn't spank me. Sometimes Christians request such a relationship, but if there is anything Christlike (or humanistic) about this, it escapes me.

Scrub = a guy who lives with parent(s), doesn't have a car, job or life outside his computer monitor. There are more scrubs – of all ages - than you might imagine.

Fluffy = a cute way of saying you are not skin and bones, but instead have a little padding on your body. "I'm not fat, I'm fluffy."

Furry = people who dress up as animals. This originated from fantasy and science fiction and now can be part of role playing. You can develop your own fursona and attend conventions. I would explain it better but I'm too removed from it to understand.

BBW = big, beautiful woman.

SSBBW = supersized big, beautiful woman. Some sources

define SSBBW as 400+.

BHM = big, handsome man.

vgl = Video Gamers League or **VGL** - Very Good Looking.

FWB - Friends with Benefits.

FFWB – Foot Friend with Benefits.

PAWG - Phat Ass White Girl

PHAT - Pretty Hot And Tempting

WOOT - Yay!! (Wow, Loot!) or Want One Of Those

WTR - Willing To Relocate.

GSOH - Good sense of humor (if you are back into the dating world, you're going to need one)

BBL = Be back later.

BRB = Be right back.

LLL = Long lingering look.

FBB = female bodybuilder.

C = Christian.

A = Asian.

G = gay.

W = white.

B = black.

H = Hispanic.

D/DF = drug and disease free.

Bi = bisexual. If he can't decide which gender he prefers, he's probably not for us.

Discrete = discreet. The good news is that someone who spells it this way probably has a computer science or mathematic education (discrete logic; finite set of values) and therefore good earning potential; the bad, he's discreet, which rhymes with deceit. Maybe you are the prudent, cautious type or are looking for a casual relationship (if there is such a thing), but I want my man to stand on top of a building, singing *The Most Beautiful Girl in the World* so everyone will know I am The One.

420 = marijuana friendly. (I had to ask someone about this.) I'm not.

Wierd = Please note that the proper spelling is w-e-i-r-d. Also keep in mind that weird is a little out of place on a profile looking for The One. (Unless you really are "wierd.")

Can or Cannot Host = Looking for sex only. If he cannot host, he probably is married or otherwise involved. Even if he can host, it appears that a few hours or minutes on hot sheets is all he is willing to offer.

1 4 3 = I love you. I would prefer hearing these three little words in person and not numerically over an electronic device (not to mention sincerely).

Love ya, luv ya = casual, friendly, not a declaration of eternal devotion. Use of "ya" instead of "you" is the tip off of an indiscriminate and wanton attitude.

404 = clueless.

Platonic = merriam-webster.com/dictionary: of, relating to, or being a relationship marked by the absence of romance or sex. In cyber world, platonic often is used by men as a cover as a bang and run. Sex, yes; going out to dinner, no; movie dates, no. See NSA.

Mouse potato = derived from couch potato; someone who spends most of his/her time online.

HMU = Hit me up (text, call or email him).

STFU = Shut the "eff" up.

WTF = What the "eff." I'd like to think that these last two would never be directed at us from a potential suitor.

4

Creating Your Profile

Your profile is your first – and often only - chance to make a lasting impression. This calls for a flattering and recent picture, fully clothed. Some women post lingerie pictures, which automatically puts her out of the running with many men. I just saw a woman's torso - red satin bra (no lace, no underwire), and dangling breasts. If she is looking to get laid, an uplift with lace would enhance her girls. If she is looking for a boyfriend, a picture of her smiling face, and/or a full body, fully dressed, shot would increase her chances. A gentleman I met over the Internet, Fake Bill, is no shrinking violet, a construction worker married and divorced three times, yet he said he would never contact a woman who put anything sexual in an Internet profile. One woman changes her photos frequently so he goes back to see what she has to offer.

Again, he loves gawking at her in her half-dressed state, but he would never, ever contact her, even for a one night stand.

Like a popular song, your ad needs a hook, something to grab interest. Alliteration such as Long Legged Lovely is fun, or should we say, lover-ly!

Don't be insulted, but here are a few basic hints:

Make sure you are posting exactly where you will be seen by those you want to attract (Woman For Man, for instance, and LTR instead of NSA) and your ad makes your objective quite clear. Don't use sex as bait if you are looking for marriage or other real relationship.

If you are posting on craigslist or other bulletin board, don't overdo it. If you post every other day, you will appear desperate.

Your picture should focus on you; no photos of you and an ex (even if his head is cropped or darkened out) or photos of you and your friends (what if he thinks one of them is more attractive than you?) and, please, absolutely none of you and your child(ren). You might feel this picture will show your love and devotion to your family and emphasize to any potential suitor that your kids are your first priority, but a predator would love to see your offspring and some decent guys will be put off by a parent unduly and unnecessarily exposing kids online.

Less is more. Keep your ad short. If you write your entire life story, even if people take the time to read it in its entirety, what will be left to talk about during the getting to know you phase? Also, the more you say, the better the chance of putting your foot in your mouth and offending someone you would have liked to have attracted.

A short bio is more intriguing than your life's true confessions. "I've been lied to, cheated on, slapped around, and supported my last man" might give Mr. Wrong the idea that you indeed could be taken advantage of – again. Most of us have figured out that Prince Charming is not on his way to rescue us and Mr. Average Nice Guy isn't looking for drama. Keep it light, friendly and cheerful. Flirty is great if you have the gift. Check any hostility at the door.

Don't admit to cheating on a former love or dating a married man. While trust is important in a relationship, full disclosure too early can frost freeze a romance before it gets the chance to blossom.

Yes, your entire ad should be light, flirty and fun! DON'T USE ALL CAPS AS IT IRRITATES PEOPLE.

Use spell check. If you aren't sure about the use of apostrophes, look up basic grammar rules. Although no man has ever complained about a woman being too smart, several have told me they contacted me because they are looking for an intelligent woman they can talk to. We can only assume "intelligent" means I can spell. On the other hand, keep in mind that many good men don't spell, type or punctuate well. Are you the grammar police or will you give a guy a little leeway?

Selecting a screen name. Your name should be descriptive of your personality of a physical attribute such as "greeneyedlady." Overtly sexual screen names can get you into trouble - or ignored.

I was sweetcaroline, which thanks to the popularity of Neil Diamond indicated my general age range and romantic streak.

After a break due to my broken heart via long-distance, I changed it to nascarbabe followed by the year of my birth. NASCAR is a passion, but it kept some men away – stock car racing is for rednecks, how can you sit and watch one continuous left turn, it's boring, it's stupid, and the implication, "YOU are stupid." Sweetcaroline was a more successful screen name.

♥ ▶▶_____

Amore

He is looking for a fishing buddy. He goes to pay lakes several times a week and if you're pretty, he'll even pay your way! Put "bait" in the subject line. ♥

Look in the mirror! Men with long, gray "hippie hair" turn me off. He could be a kind-hearted veterinarian who loves to hike, but if he looks like a straggler from the 60s, he will not look good to me. What do (did) I have to offer? Long, graying hippie hair! A little layering, and a box of strawberry blonde hair coloring and back to the 21st century I bounced. Choppy and sexy, the Shag is back in style. If you don't have the time or money for a salon session, you can shape your hair yourself. There are instructions on the Internet, but I put my hair into a ponytail on top of my head and cut off several inches. Viola! A shag! Casual, tousled, kittenish – youthful and fun!

Check out craigslist to become a model to showcase a stylist's talents. You have limited input on the design of your new 'do, but it's still a great opportunity to update your look. Free.

We have heard many times that a profile with pictures gets at least eight times as many responses as one without. Presumably, you should use flattering photos. Flattering recent pictures, it must be emphasized, not from days of yore. After a younger-thinner fiasco, I learned my lesson, determined to offer an accurate representation of myself to any and all potential beaus. I hate getting my picture taken, and any extra weight tends to accumulate in a pad underneath my chin (and on my stomach, if you must know). A friend offered a little advice that sounded good at the time. Her former husband has "no" neck so he sticks his head straight out ("like this" as she demonstrated his trick). The pictures a friend took of me demonstrating this pose show a woman desperately trying to look like a turtle or not look like a turtle, I couldn't tell which. Although I will always wish I had the money for liposuction, every time I read about another death from plastic surgery/lipo gone wrong, I count my blessings as a non-rich person.

Immediately before a photo session, my daughter did a show and tell of blending eye shadow. She learned the foundations of foundation from her mother, but continued in independent study to be a Ph.D. of cosmetic wizardry.   Practice! Blend!! This is a symphony! My eyebrows are too thin and I look tired. Smile!

Even though she is beautiful, and young, and has flattering while genuine photos posted, until recently my daughter has had the same miserable luck with Internet dating as her mother.

However, it's a numbers game and all it takes is one. The One.

A blouse, dress or sweater in a solid color, preferably "your" color will frame your face.

A request for a full-length photo is fair. Cheat a little with heels and dark jeans or black skirt and hose.

Since my hair is flat (my mother always hated to get her picture taken, saying that her head was flat), I am interested in a beehive comb currently advertised on tv. No backcombing or teasing needed to give your hair that flirty look.

My friend Megan uses whitening strips and her teeth look movie star bright! I bought some but when I read the disclaimer about loose teeth or less than perfect gums, I gave them away. What if one of my teeth came out?! My slightly off white but clean smile with minty fresh breath will have to do.

You most likely aren't a comedienne, so perhaps you could reconsider posting a picture of you sticking out your tongue or crossing your eyes do or posing in any other cute position. While Jenny McCarthy could get away with it, she is probably not posting her profile online.

Since you are posting your photo, it is not necessary for you to make comments about your appearance such as "pretty" or "slightly overweight." Let the viewer be the judge of what he finds attractive, fat, pretty...

Please don't cheat by using an old photo or God forbid, someone else's picture. One man was particularly upset when he found out the picture of the woman he fell in love with online was in actuality the woman's daughter. And even the daughter's picture was old, because the daughter had put on considerable weight since it had been taken.

Although my profile pictures have included one showing me years younger and pounds lighter, and one with me wearing a red Dale Earnhardt, Jr. jacket and a large red velvet rose in my hair, and one with my arms around my Rottweiler Sweetie, and one with me wearing a t-shirt from a sparkplug company standing in a field of native lilies (the tall orange tigers seen in every ditch, every June, in rural areas of the Midwest), I nonetheless (hypocritically) was put off by the posturings and posings of several men.

One guy, dressed in farmer-type cover-alls (this could also be a railroad engineer's uniform) and railroad engineer's hat pointed to magazine at the left side of his face and laughed.

Perhaps he is in his basement, playing with his Lionel, pretending it is chugging up mountains, or maybe he is involved with a scenic railway. For all we know, he could be a real railroad engineer. My daughter asked for, and received, a Snoopy train set last Christmas.

She will kill me for saying this, but she will never see twenty again. Her nephews/my grandsons and I were all very envious of this particular delivery from the Santa Express.

But what is cute for a younger woman can be odd for an older man.

All aboard the crazy train commonly known as The Internet Express!!!! We'll speed up and steam through Bitter Springs, without slowing, then stop in both Love and Inspiration, Arizona; Elephant Butte Lake State Park, New Mexico, might be fun, but nothing serious; up to Loveland and Sugar City, Colorado; bypassing Wanker's Corner, Oregon, down through Hookers' Corner, Indiana, we go to Big Bone Lick, Kentucky (just miles from Rabbit Hash), then on to Sweet Lips, Tennessee.

We stop for a quick stay in Friendship, Arkansas before heading to Kissimmee, Florida then double back to Valentine, Nebraska where we'll all live happily ever after.

Another suitor sent me a photo of himself wearing a t-shirt and short cotton shorts perched on a crotch rocket. Unfortunately, he looked like a former in-law. I don't know why he contacted me of all women because "no pets" was one of his mandatory requirements. I confess I sent the picture to my kids, telling them they might have a new dad on the way, one who looked just like Grandpa! "Sweet!" (sarcasm runs through our bloodline) replied one of them, who shall remain nameless.

Another wore a Budweiser t-shirt coordinating with his screen name, "wannashareabeer." No, I don't want to drink with him or anyone else whose only interest seems to be found in an aluminum can or brown bottle. He was cuter than the average fifty-seven year old man, though. (He was Gemini and they do tend to stay younger longer.)

I've paid subscription fees to dating sites and met guys, and I've also not met anyone on paying sites. Now I stick with free sites.

A particularly expensive (about $50 a month) site markets itself as the ultimate in compatibility matching. One man I talked with through a free site liked my picture and emailed me. He was having a problem with his current girlfriend and trying to decide if he should keep dating her or move on, hence his joining another site. He was raising his seven year old granddaughter and the girlfriend didn't like kids, didn't want to be bothered, and was quite rude and rejecting to the grandchild. They argued about this every week-end. However, these two people were matched as each other's top compatible partner, and he eventually decided to stay in the relationship. (The sex must have been good, or more likely, it was better than nothing.) Since we spent little time emailing each other and had never spoken on the phone, I had no conflict of interest in stating the supremely obvious, "If you are raising a grandchild and she doesn't like kids, you are not compatible." He took the test results as Gospel, and I never heard from him again. The poor grandchild!!!

❤ ►►

Amore

Jeremiah is looking for a Bible study buddy, in person or by phone, email or text. If this leads to a romantic relationship, then it is the Lord's will. ❤

Press hysteria aside, not one man has been dangerous, violent, or scary. Most were not after my money, probably because I have none.

If your search criteria is too narrow, you won't get as many responses, and you might miss out on The Love of Your Life. Does he really have to be at least 6' tall? Is his eye or hair color a deal-breaker? Decide what is truly important to you (no drug use, for example, unless you want someone to share "420" times). If an athletic body type is critical to your wants and needs, you may exclude men with "a few extra pounds." Unless you are footloose and fancy free, it is wise to stay within a hundred or so miles of where you lay your head at night.

If you ask for more than you can put on the table – good looks or high income when you are in the average range – you are going to be disappointed.

We might take this advice seriously: "Please, please stop saying 'I'm no Barbie.' We know that! We're lucky if you look like Roseanne Barr on her worst day. 99.9999% of women do not look like Barbie and women who do don't need to use the personals to find a man."

This girl might have unrealistic expectations. She's a BBW looking for a combination of James Dean, Romeo, and the guy who starred as Bruno. She wants someone responsible yet not serious, someone who will listen to her for hours, and playful yet serious.

Another BBW is single mom looking for a good man. No BHM need apply.

Keep it positive!! Another "competitor" in Cyber Love spent two paragraphs describing her basement pool table and as for herself, she said she was overweight, but losing, something I would never say. (We are already perfect!) We are what we are today, and let tomorrow take care of itself. It also sounds like you are trying too hard. In addition, she mentioned the property she owns and that her best friend, her mother, lives with her. Dating is similar to interviewing for a job, in that there are many candidates, and therefore people are looking for reasons to exclude possibilities. You don't want to be weeded out before the first round, do you? You also do not want a fortune hunter stealing your heart, and your bank account. So, leave out your living arrangements and your possessions. That is your business and has nothing to do with going out on a casual date. Not to mention that a good relationship starts out with a casual date and keeps growing, unless of course we are lucky enough to be struck by the Thunderbolt, otherwise known as Love at First Sight.

MISTAKE ONE was so bad that it needs to be mentioned yet again. Confessions – along with an excuse and atonement – of

a fudging online poster.

There is no defense for what I did, other than "everyone else does it." Mitigating circumstances could be that I was in a bad place, having recently buried my husband and drowning my sorrow with sugary treats. I always make sure I am on the other side of the camera whenever possible so there were very few good shots of me. You may want to learn from my poor attempt at seduction and sleight of hand when I posted a picture at least five years old (and many pounds thinner).

However, after being left standing in a restaurant by a man who responded to my We Must Have Missed Each Other email by bluntly stating it was no mistake, that I had misrepresented myself, I cried, felt sorry for myself for several days, blamed him for being superficial, and then tossed out every sugary drink in the house, and eventually lost forty pounds. A recent physical revealed excellent blood sugar levels and I credit that "cruel" man for that. All is well that ends well.

5

Be the Best You Can Be

Before you jump back into dating, it wouldn't hurt to spend some time on getting to know you, yourself.

If you don't know what you like, dislike, need, desire, deserve, how on earth can you chose a significant other?

Think about past relationships, and if you don't have a lot of dating experience, think about guys you've wanted to date. What about them was so attractive?

Most probably you will attract men who are like you. Your education level, your looks, your total package all work for you. If you want someone with an advanced education, call the nearest college and enroll, if for only one class.

You want a man who dresses well? Get thee to a bookstore or library and stock up on fashion magazines. Visit upscale department stores and try on the high end merchandise, checking the clearance racks. Stop for a free make-over on the way out.

If the man of your dreams is fit and toned, hit the trail!

It goes without saying if you rush home from work, make your dinner and veg out in front of the tv, you are more likely to stay single. Yes, it takes effort and energy to go out and see the world, but even if you only touch up your make-up and go to the grocery, you will see and be seen.

By doing a little work on your life, you will be able to attract the best person for you.

These are common sense suggestions, so don't be offended by a simplistic approach.

Believe you deserve the best out of life. Invest in yourself and your future by getting and/or continuing an education. By keeping up with the latest technology, you will be employable. Even if you marry a wealthy man and do not need to work, you will always know that you can take care of yourself. Independence is an attractive quality.

You probably don't want to become a Mountain Woman, but developing self-sufficiency will serve you well. Can you change a tire? I can't, but I have roadside assistance with my phone contract. Do you know how to use a hammer and nails? I don't, but I am able to set a humane trap and transport marauding raccoons that otherwise would destroy my yard, attack my cats and attempt to break into my house.

By necessity, I learned how to replace the plastic pipes under my sink (my plumber was too fat to bend over so I had to do it myself) and hook up the hoses to my aging above the ground pool keep it clean enough for water walking, and then close it each fall. However, if I had the money I would hire someone to help with housecleaning. Keeping house is beyond my capabilities.

Eat well, exercise, get adequate sleep, don't smoke, drink moderately or not at all, leave drugs alone, take care of yourself in every way possible. Read fashion magazines. You don't need to dress like a fashionista or have a closet full of expensive clothing to look your best. Learn what flatters your figure. Wear make-up even when you take out the trash. Maintain your health and hygiene so that you are comfortable in your own skin.

To intrigue a man, mix things up a bit. If you are Sally Sensible, leave a slightly sexy magazine casually on your coffee table (or night stand, if you are to that point). Conversely, if you are Ms. Sexy Siren, leave a traditional homemaking magazine for him to "casually" notice. A serious novel or how-to book would also make a good impression. (No, you don't have to read it, but would it kill you?)

Easy exercise (physical & mental). If you live or work within walking distance of a library, hurry on down and check out some books. Balance them between two bags and carry them back, taking a detour if you have time. You are walking with weights! You also have something to enrich your mind, if you so chose. The rare man in my bedroom will see a book on serial killers next to one on gardening (these are my relaxation), but I hide the relationship books. Don't want him to get the wrong idea about me! (That's a joke...)

Learn a new skill. It doesn't matter what. Mastering something unusual or not practical to your everyday life can enrich your life. Stained glass? Dress making? Decoupage? Jewelry design? Gravestone rubbing? Photography? Magic tricks? Learn a foreign language? Belly dancing? Tarot reading? Sky diving? Geocaching?

Brush up on your cooking and baking skills. You don't have to rival Aunt Bea or Martha but you can develop your own specialties. Perhaps you could create healthy and tasty dishes that would endear you to Mr. Right. Since many men prefer plain home cooking, build up a repertoire of easy menus. If you are after a gourmet, there are many books and magazines and online sources.

For your health's sake, organize and plan your meals so every day you'll have four to five servings of fruit and the same number of vegetables. I cheat and eat mostly fruits and fewer vegetables but it still beats fast food, grease and salt.

6

Your Profile Heading (also known as a Scarehead)

Conventional wisdom states that a hook is second only to a photograph in capturing interest. Many people won't spend more than a few seconds before going to the next available applicant. Creative, cute or downright disgusting, these headings from around the country caught my eye.

Men

- Want to Start Things With a Bang!
- Can I get you pregnant??? (Oddly, this is more common that you might suspect)
- I need a girlfriend ... Please start spending my money today ... LOL
- Looking for my very own black hollyhock
- Grandpa (72) is looking for his baby girl
- I bang [he actually used a much stronger word] as if I have to prove something to the world
- NSA. Just once time, no LTR – and no money
- Let Me Teach You Dirty Words In Arabic!

- We'll play, I'll pay, then be on my way
- ISO Last First Date [another common sentiment]
- Are you perfectly imperfect?
- Clark Kent seeks Louis Lane [yep, he probably meant "Lois"]
- Noon time make out??
- I'll be your Handyman!
- Sugardaddy ISO a girl with a small waist, large hips and a delicious bubblebutt [not me].
- You be my sunny day and I'll be your shade tree
- We all have baggage so let's unpack!
- We Can Lie About How We Met
- Into k9? [I love my dog but not in that way]
- Electrician starts lots of sparks!
- One house broken male, free to a good home
- The only reason I'm single is because she cheated on me
- Don't smoke weed with Willie
- Free orgasms
- Are you a squirter??? [this is another common theme throughout the United States]
- Married chick for strip club fun?
- Fat Chicks Rock!!
- Want to share my snuggie?
- A fat penguin for you [I read the entire ad but still don't understand it.]
- Insert Cute, Catchy Title Here [this is everywhere]

- Older Man Will Share Tranquility in the Garden

Women
- Alice seeking Mad Hatter
- Looking for a white guy with dreadlocks
- We're pirates and the moon is full
- Looking for a husband to take care of me [aren't we all?]
- Damsel needs to feel loved and safe
- Please put the name of your favorite truck in the subject line
- I deleted all my social networks and now I have no friends
- Are only good looking people allowed on here?
- I am not Barbie
- Your birthday is April 8 -26 [since it spans two astrological signs it doesn't make sense to me]
- Talk nerdy to me
- My dogs think I should get a life
- Where are all the fun, sexy guys over 50? [yeah, where?]
- Drive me wild with your Hasidic tzitzit and peyos
- Sissy white bitch [male] to serve ebony goddess
- Are you the macaroni to my cheese?
- If you think Adele is hot…
- Have Life, Will Share
- I Want, I Want, I Want, I Need, I Need, I Need
- I want a man, not another little boy [this is another common theme]
- Amazingly Amazing

- Punk, poetry, Pacific highway
- There are worse things in the world than being fat [there certainly are!]
- Housework in high heels
- Let's log off and grab a beer!
- I'm fat and ugly
- Why don't more men smile in their pictures?
- Cinnamon Apple Crunch
- Looking for a good looking man who's obsessed by inner beauty

7

A Sample Questionnaire

Marital status:
- Single?
- Divorced?
- Separated (for real, not just wishful thinking; your partner is aware that you are indeed no longer together)?
- Widowed?
- Living with a Romantic Partner?
- Married?
- It's complicated?

   If you are already involved why are you on a dating site? Are you emotionally available?

   If your romantic life is already complicated why are you looking for more entanglement(s)?

Height:

Weight:

Eye color:

Ethnic background:

- Black
- Caucasian
- Native American
- Hispanic
- Middle Eastern
- Asian
- Mixed Race

Do you date outside your race?

Hair color:

- Black
- Brown
- Red
- Blond/blonde
- Gray
- Mixed color
- Bald

Hair length:

- Pixie cut
- Short
- Medium
- Shoulder length
- Long

Men only (we hope):

- Clean shaven
- Mustache

- Soul Patch [so sexy!]
- Beard
- Shaved head

Body type:
- Slender
- Athletic
- Average
- A Few Extra Pounds
- Curvaceous
- Hourglass
- Husky/BHM
- Body builder
- BBW

A personal note: Be careful if you call yourself athletic. This past year I participated in metro parks sponsored Winter Hikes, some of them over rugged terrain (and none of them for the 50 and up crowd). Although I was able to keep up with the group it was a struggle when trudging up steep snow covered hills. However, being overly impressed with my physical abilities, I signed up for a rock climbing class and then was hit in the head by reality when the harnesses for women were too small to cradle my core. Looking around, I was struck by how thin everyone else was. I am not the M3PW, but I still carry "a few extra pounds." I left, not humiliated (I'm past that), but disappointed. Motivated I am, athletic and toned I am not.

Personal habits:

- Do you smoke?
  - No
  - Socially
  - Daily
- Would you date a smoker?

Drug use:
- Absolutely not
- 420 friendly
- Socially
- Often

Alcohol
- No
- Socially
- Love it
- I'll explain later

Music:
- Acid rock
- Adult contemporary
- Alternative
- Rock and roll
- Bebop
- Big bands [I've always loved Ol' Blue Eyes but only as a solo artist]
- Rhythm and blues
- Doo wop

- Soul
- Blue grass
- Blue eyed soul [how I would love to meet someone who would inspire me to listen to *Soul and Inspiration*]
- Calypso
- Christian [including, oddly enough, Christian hip hop, Christian metal and Christian punk]
- Classic country
- Classic rock
- Country rock
- Dance [as Phil Collins sang, *I Can't Dance*]
- Disco [I love the Bee Gees but consider their non-disco their best body of work]
- Dixieland Jazz
- Easy listening [depending on my mood it soothes me, or makes me feel homicidal]
- Emo
- Rap [other than the occasional Kid Rock tune, count me out]
- Folk
- Gospel [I don't listen but my dad sang Gospel before I was born]
- Heavy metal [I am a fan by blood – my son listened to it growing up]
- A mix of rockabilly, swamp pop, R&B, and country, otherwise known as Credence Clearwater Revival [you might want to reconsider your romance if *Bad Moon Risin'*

plays comes on the radio when you are on your first date]
- Honky tonk [really? in 2012? could be fun, though]
- Reggae
- Latino [She Bangs! She Bangs!]
- New age
- Motown [even though this genre is technically oldie, I never tire of it]
- Oldies [for some reason it irritates me when guy lists this as his favorite music]
- Outlaw country [Waylon, Willie and the boys]
-]Sweet soul music [yeah, yeah, I do like good music)

Can a Metallica aficionado and a Josh Groban devotee live happily ever after? Sure! (But it might work better if the guy is the head banger and the girl, a popera fan instead of vice versa).

Religion:
- Christian-Protestant
- Christian-Catholic
- Christian-Fundamentalist
- Jewish
- Buddist
- Muslim
- New Age
- Regularly attend church/religious services
- Attend services on holidays only
- Not religious but spiritual

- Not religious

Are you willing to date outside your religion? If not religious would you date someone who was? How important is your religion?

Personality traits:
- Open to new ideas and experiences
- Conservative, traditional
- Believe in being prepared, always on time, pay attention to detail, neat and orderly
- Financially responsible
- Chronic financial difficulties
    - It's the economy's fault
    - Perhaps a personal budget overhaul is order
- Spontaneous, impulsive
- Messy, don't keep things in order
- Extrovert
    - Life of the party
    - Will talk to anyone, anywhere
- Introvert
- Compassionate and cooperative
    - Considerate
    - Friendly
    - Generous
    - Helpful
    - Willing to compromise

- - Optimistic about people
- Self-absorbed
  - Not overly interested in others' problems
  - Can come off as insulting or condescending
- Moody
- Argumentative [or would you instead prefer " liking a good debate?"]
- Stubborn
- Opinionated
- Easily irritated, stressed out and upset
- Depressed
- Worried

Do you have a car?

Do you have your own house or apartment? Live with parents? Roommates?

Do you have children?
- Yes – under 18, live with me
- Yes – under 18, live with other parent
- Yes – under 18, shared parenting
- Yes – over 18/out of the house/independent
- Yes – over 18, live with me
- No

Do you want children?
- Yes
- No

- Haven't decided

Will you date someone with children?
- Yes
- No

Employment:
- Professional
- Blue collar
- Office
- Unemployed
- Disabled
- Retired
- Not a high priority

Income:

One question I always leave unanswered is income and prefer others do, too. I'd rather see no information than a blatant lie. It's no one's business, and you run the risk of scaring off some men (whether too low or too high for their individual needs) or drawing in a fortune hunter. It's fun to have someone interested in your ass, but not your assets.

Education:
- High school
- Some college
- Associates degree
- Bachelors degree

- Masters degree
- Post graduate
    - PhD
    - M.D.
    - J.D.

If you have attended even one college class, "some college" is acceptable. If you have no college credits, do not state "college graduate" or even "some college." Even if you feel you have life experience equal to a college degree (and many of us do), there is no GED for college. Please don't get caught in a lie. This is much worse than posting an older photo (aka "everyone does it") and we all know what cheating on your true appearance does to a budding romance.

Do you have pets?
- No and I don't want to date anyone who does
- No – I am allergic
- No – but I like other people's pets
- Yes – dog
- Yes – cat
- Yes – bird
- Yes – horse
- Yes – a menagerie (too many to count)
- Yes – other

Safety first! Do not include your name, address or phone

number.

Describe yourself. What sets you apart from the crowd? Your taste in music, magazines, books, and hobbies are what make you a loveable unique individual. What are your goals? Are you ambitious?

Be organized! I'm not, but a friend who shared her system with me certainly is. Emily bought a three ring binder, five inches thick, along with divider tabs and enough inkjet paper to paper her dorm room so that she could print out and save all chat sessions and personal notations about each suitor. She flew to the East Coast to spend a week-end on a boat with Ryan and although the relationship didn't last she treasured their time together. They had fun, but he wasn't The One.

She also wasted time with a much older man who "drank a bit" and was seeing Diane, a woman older than Emily but younger than Norman. What Keyboard Cassanova didn't realize was that Emily also was attracted to women and that one week-end when he wasn't available, in the ultimate eff you Emily and Diane teamed up for a romantic romp of their own. Emily dumped Norman and assumed Diane did, too, but she wasn't sure because she blocked both from her life. What do you think? Norman probably weaseled his way back into Diane's life.

Shortly after, Emily met Alfonso through an online dating service and after a whirlwind courtship he relocated to be with her, they married and started a family.

Hmmmm. Would Emily been happier with a fifty-five year old alkie who had no desire to change any part of his lifestyle or a thirty year old Latin lover who was willing to commit everything he had to building a relationship with her?

Lesson learned. Organization is great, but never selling yourself short is the most important part of dating – and living.

8

Questions He Might Ask – Know Thyself

What is your favorite dining experience?
- Steak house
- Red Lobster
- 50s diner
- Home cookin' hole in the wall/greasy spoon [yummy!]
- Olive Garden
- Trendy bistro
- Applebees

Saturday night pleasure:
- Bar
- Dance club
- Sporting event
- With friends
- Home with a good movie and pizza
- Online, of course!

According to my friends, I am:
- Quiet and thoughtful
- Lively and fun
- A great catch – why am I still single?
- Cautious and conservative

I'm still single because:
- I'm picky
- I've been married before
- All the good ones are already taken
- My career is my life
- I don't have time to date
- He cheated on me
- All men are bastards
- I'm painfully shy
- I have a fatal flaw or two
- I'm not single

The perfect romantic getaway:
- Cuddled up in a cabin in the woods
- Vegas, baby!
- Home in our jammies watching *Family Guy*
- Skiing
- Daytona 500, live and in person
- Bright lights in the City that Never Sleeps
- Paris

- A cottage on the beach
- An amusement park
- The zoo

My level of fitness:
- I need to hit the gym and/or hiking trail
- I'm perfect!
- I'm good
- Sexy is as sexy does
- Yuck – exercise makes me sweat
- I'm cerebral and I don't care
- I'm not particularly brainy and I still don't care about working out
- I love nothing better than watching tv with a plate of chicken tenders and a bag of chips, downed with a cold one

My ideal guy:
- A cowboy – rugged and an outdoor lover
- Athletic
- Outgoing
- Supportive
- Curious
- Subdued
- At peace with his life as it is
- Adventurous
- Brave, courageous, bold

- Secure
- Dependable
- Family oriented
- Successful
- Honest
- Reserved
- Sophisticated
- Studious and scholarly
- All of the above
- Keyboard Romeo (just kidding, but you have a great chance of meeting one)

Favorite Outdoor Activities:
- Kyaking, canoeing in the wilderness
- Boating on a cabin cruiser
- Sitting on the dock with a Margarita
- Outdoors? Are you kidding? Give me a luxury suite!
- Ziplining (my daughter-in-law, God bless her heart, suggested that I might enjoy this – me, who is afraid of heights, me, who couldn't fit into a harness to learn rock climbing – but if I had the cajones to try I probably would)
- Rappelling down a mountain
- "Pull!" – clay pigeon shooting
- Hot air ballooning
- Parachuting
- Horseback riding

- Mushroom hunting
- Tromping through the woods to find abandoned mines and haunted railroad tunnels [my idea of a good time]
- Hiking through old graveyards looking for interesting stones [my idea of a good time, part two]
- Hunting
- Fishing
- Riding through the countryside on the back of a motorcycle or inside a red hot convertible [convertible gets my vote, but it seems there are a lot more motorcycle owners than soft tops]
- Bicycling

Remember that these should be actual interests or things you are willing to try, not just castles in the air fantasies. Otherwise, you might find yourself screaming down a mountain (terrified), hiking up an incline (complaining that your feet hurt), worried about running into ghosts, or baiting a hook with a real live worm (yuck).

Several men have told me that women have told them that they like hiking, cycling, and other active sports, but when they meet the women in question, she is severely out of shape and obviously does not hike or cycle or do anything else that takes active participation.

One man asked a woman point blank: Why did you say you hike? "Well, I would like to..." You can't pretend to be someone other than the real you. Would you like a man to blatantly lie about his interests?

Sense of Humor:

- Urbane, sophisticated
- Dry, droll
- Sarcastic
- Knee slapping
- Ironic
- Pundit
- Wisecracks – the Queen or King of one liners
- Witty
- Self deprecating
- Bathroom, off color [keep it to yourself until you are sure it is appreciated and keep in mind that it may never be]
- Ridiculing others [keep it to yourself, permanently]
- Saturday Night Live
- Long live Barney Fife!
- Slapstick
- Dumb, dumber, dumbest
- Git 'er done!
- Easily entertained by Hee Haw reruns
- What business is it of yours what I think is funny?

One of the hardest questions to answer when talking to a potential date is "What do you like to do in your spare time?"

What spare time? Do reading and watch tv count? How interesting is that?

An honest assessment of my fair market value:
- I am over 50
- I have never learned to keep house
- I love to cook
- I'm learning financial responsibility
- I drive a 5 on the floor
- I love to cook
- My family is the most important part of my life
- I am not a bitch [I consider this a liability since it seems most men like 'em]
- I am low maintenance [ditto on this being a liability in some men's eyes]
- I am a hard worker
- I love to learn
- I have never learned to keep house [this deserves two mentions]
- I want to be Martha Stewart when I grow up
- I love animals
- Even when I was 20 I didn't have a hard body
- I like most people
- I love music
- I'm getting much needed dental work done
- I love gardening
- I love day trips and little adventures
- I can't swim but spend as much time in the pool as possible

- I like believing in ghosts
- I am not a night person
- I don't drink
- I don't need a man, but I sure would like to have one of my very own
- On the other hand, I don't want drama and in the past I have been insecure
- I recycle

9

Keeping Your Sanity While Using Insane Dating Method

Don't check his profile to see if he is still "single" after you are dating or even just talking about meeting. Do you want to get hurt? He will tell you when he wants to be exclusive, and he might never want to commit to you. This is a harsh statement, but meant to keep you grounded. Although there are many guys who are sincere and looking for just one woman, there are professional daters as well as keyboard Romeos who have no intention of meeting anyone.

Proceed "as if" you are single even if you are madly in love with your Internet suitor. Rushing into a physical relationship can lead to heartbreak.

To protect yourself, date and talk to many guys, and don't have sex with any.

Do you have a webcam? Have you been talked into cyber sex? Do you wear lingerie while conducting this torrid affair? Did you ever consider he might be chatting with other women at the very same time? He might be viewing porn. How do I know this?

Once (fully dressed) while chatting with the London cop,

out of the blue he typed, "Is she gay?"

I thought we were discussing his endless love, desire, and admiration of *moi*, but he hastily apologized and explained he was also chatting with a "cousin" and sent the wrong message to the wrong person. Indeed! Fortunately, my daughter called and wanted to go shopping, right that instance, requiring me to log off. Had she not called with that message, I would have called her to suggest an immediate shopping excursion. The next time we IM'd he was more careful, and so was I.

If you do decide to IM in front of a webcam, you will want to treat it as a real date! If you want him to consider you as a romantic partner instead of a time filler, have freshly shampooed hair, flattering make-up, and an attractive outfit. OK, even lingerie if that's what you want. But no sloppy sweatshirts or unkempt hair! If he is so uninspiring that your appearance truly does not matter, you might consider whether you might have better ways to use your time.

Webcams also require a neat and orderly background. Hanging a sheet behind you will hide any clutter as well as keep the focus on what's important – YOU.

But please keep it in mind that by having cybersex, it is less likely that you will ever have real sex with your Internet love.

But if hot sex with a man miles away is what you want, enjoy! A lacy push-up bra is a great start, and with bronzer applied on the sides of your breasts, you can create a shadow that will suggest cleavage an additional cup size. Spritz on cologne, and sip your favorite beverage.

Red nail polish will get his blood going in the right direction, too.

Remember in old movies when the heroine would oh so demurely undress behind a folding screen, draping her discarded clothing over the top? How about a pair of barely there panties in a size or two smaller "casually" tossed in the background?

Now you have my blood going! But we had to talk about cybersex, didn't we?

10

Big Beautiful Women

Are you a Big Beautiful Woman? Should you spell it out in your ad? Instead of depicting yourself as a BBW, why not take care of yourself and emphasize your gorgeous, attractive, alluring, appealing, angelic, enticing, lovely, graceful, stunning, bewitching, exquisite and fascinating qualities? Post a picture and let him decide if he finds you attractive.

Full-figured, Rubenesque, fluffy, queen sized, plus sized, what does it matter? Size is subjective. Proof? A male friend once described Ashley Judd as "full figured". He was a huge fan, and no, he didn't confuse the tiny waisted star of *Kiss the Girls* with anyone else.

Voluptuous and zaftig are associated with sensuality and ripeness. Soft, feminine hair, artfully applied make-up, flattering clothing, light cologne – beautiful you.

This from Cousin Gene - don't wear your hair too short. "From the back you look like you've gained a good 15 pounds."

What he really said was, "I never realized your butt was that big." I must have weighed all of 120.

Exposed! The Myth of the 300 Pound Woman Deflated! Well, not exactly. According to my non-scientific research (a 27 year old man), many women do post older/unrealistic photos and stats, then show up for the date. Patrick goes through with the date, but never contacts the woman again, not because of her weight, but because of the lie. Several men have told me stories about the Mythical 300 Pound Woman. One guy drives past the restaurant or movie theatre where they arranged their first meeting, and if the M3PW is standing in front, he guns his engine and speeds away.

Don't be a Big Beautiful Woman – be a big Beautiful Woman. Minimize the big, and maximize your beauty and femininity. Your curves are lavish and luscious. You are a loving, warm-hearted soft bodied woman. Learn how to use make-up to enhance and access your most beautiful features. Wear clothing in flattering colors. Eat healthy foods and exercise.   If you make the most of your appearance, you will never be The Mythical 300 Pound Woman, no matter what you weigh.

Although black is slimming, you might want to consider wearing a monochrome outfit in a bright color. Pink is a good choice: romantic, girly, and flattering to most complexions.

I've lied about my weight, too, and been humiliated, so perhaps I am in the annals of 300 Pound Woman history. The most I ever weighed was close to 200, but some men like skinny (or as one put it, "skinnie minnie's" - the ubiquitous use of inappropriate apostrophes is part of Cyberworld). If you are a 300 Pound Woman, don't get your panties in a bunch, because many men enjoy a larger woman. Make the most of your appearance, smile, and don't apologize.

11

Widowers, Looking for Replacement Wives

It's understandable. A man has been married to the same woman for twenty or thirty years and built a comfortable life with her. She dies. The kids have flown the nest, and in some cases it is a fine fluffy snuggery indeed. It might even be paid off. He doesn't want to pick up stakes and start over, so he advertises for Wife #2 (or #3 in case the dead wife's replacement didn't work out).

Widowers and I aren't a good match. I have a home, which although in need of TLC, is important to me. Most of the widowers in my age bracket are retired, and I work two jobs. I don't want to stay home and entertain a man, and I feel the need to stay self-sufficient. One man has already dropped dead on me, leaving me financially frightened. It could happen again. A divorce would be a good possibility also, after the widower realizes that unlike his sentimental remembrances of Wife #1, I am no angel.

One wanted me to move three hours away, emailing me pictures of his home. Her cookbooks were still where she left them.

We know all how much a little woman likes to cook and who could ask for more than a fully furnished kitchen. Perhaps you could. I know I want more out of life than living in a nicer house and being Chief Cook and Bottle Washer, not that I am qualified to be the next Mrs. Homemaker even if I wanted to fill that vacancy.

After talking to or going on out an exploratory date with several widowers, I will give them a 100% rating for the ability and desire to provide for a mate.

Can you love this man? Will you love him with everything you have? He's already had his heart broken. Can you respect him? Gratitude would be a little too much, as it smacks of the opposite of love.

If you need a home, a widower could be perfect for you. If you are a woman who loves keeping house, there is probably an opening for you. Just don't be obvious about it.

Can you live in the shadow of a ghost? One who might be considered a saint? Perhaps a celestial being who left children who may or may not be ecstatic to see dear old dad happily remarried?

However, if you do decide to retire and/or rely solely on a man's largesse, please keep a few things in mind. He might have made provisions for his pension to be paid solely to him, and upon his death, the annuity stops. He might be miserly. He might be used to being in control. He might leave everything to his children. If your husband left you an annuity, make sure marriage to another man will not affect it.

Widowers in general aren't a good match for me. The ones I talked to all seemed too serious about life, all claimed to have been married to saints, whom they treated like princesses at all times.

Not Even Spellcheck Would Help

Several widowers have regretfully posted that their wives "pasted away." ☹

Perry called me several times, and each conversation eventually turned to the night his wife died. It was sad to hear about high school sweethearts being separated thirty years later by cancer. Although I knew it couldn't work for us, he was nice enough that I would be concerned that Ms. Wrong would take advantage of his vulnerabilities. He was a plant manager, and owned a nice house. How did I know we weren't for each other? He lived about four hours away, and any woman would have to relocate to his home. I felt I would be a stand-in or understudy finally getting her big break. Perry had three hobbies: bass fishing, bowling, and boating. He competes in fishing tournaments, which would have been a new experience for me. He bowls twice a week, and as a stand-in I would be expected to join his league. I can't bowl! I don't want to learn! Boating would be great, but he wanted the stand-in to spend every Friday night through Sunday afternoon weather permitting as his first mate. What about my family? What about my house and yard? What about my life? I'm seriously land-locked and although I love the water, I could not drive four hours each way to Lake Erie and spend every week-end on a boat!! Weekends are for shopping, cleaning, reading, gardening, hiking, seeing my family!!!

Theodore had been widowed for several years by the time we met. He took early retirement, doesn't do any volunteer work, and has no hobbies other than watching *Bonanza*. After I came home from a stressful day at work, would discussing the escapades of Little Joe, Hoss, Ben and Hop Sing be enough to keep us together? He has a routine and does not venture out of his comfort zone. When he mentioned he would like a black lab, I gave him the name of a local rescue group that had several socialized, neutered, and vaccinated retrievers. Although Theodore liked the idea of getting a pound puppy, "I will not pay for a stray dog." He would not consider that he would be paying a fraction of what a veterinarian would charge for necessary preventative veterinary care, so I would not consider dating him.

Theodore answered another ad that I placed a few weeks later. Guess what? This time around he is very adaptable and enjoys many activities, including hiking. (No mention of *Bonanza*.)

Leonard waited (almost) an entire month after his bereavement before diving back into the dating pool, and although it is said that everyone grieves differently, he didn't seem to be suffering. He was very disappointed that I wanted to go out to eat and that I was fully clothed. After he got home he emailed me saying that he had hoped I had nothing on under my dress as he would have enjoyed groping me. I never heard from him again, yet another piece of evidence proving the existence of God. On the up side, I can't imagine that he would compare a new honey to his sainted wife as she appears to be Ancient History.

One widower I used to chat with told me he kept his wife's clothes in the closet, and when he missed her he went in, shut the door and inhaled her perfume. One of my husband's shirts waits for him in my clothes closet, and when I smell motor oil on anyone else I think of my husband, so it was easy for me to be understanding. He was very intelligent and obviously not ready to "move on." He also said that many women would tell him that they would make him forget his wife and he appreciated the fact that I did not.

Dwight professed to be a retired professor, the widower of a registered nurse. We agreed to meet at pizzeria for lunch, and although I was on time, Dwight had already polished off two-thirds of the pizza, leaving one piece on a paper plate which he shoved toward me as I sat down. "It's yours" was his first statement to me; "A man can cover an extra twenty pounds by wearing a suit, but there's no way a woman can hide hers" was his second. His black suit appeared to be attempting to conceal a good fifty to seventy pounds, but I didn't have much to say. His moustache was clearly dyed to match the dead squirrel on his head which I watched wobble and wiggle as he continued eating and talking. He wasn't very old, perhaps mid to late fifties, but it appeared he was dependent on dentures that he must have left at home. Dwight confided (or bragged) that he had been banned from a local grocery chain as other customers complained that his birds perching on the grocery carts' were unsanitary. However, he now frequents another chain and so far has had no problems. He was easy to lose: My cats really love birds. (So do I, but this half-truth was expedient.) Also, I fear I was not attractive enough for him. As I scampered out of the restaurant he polished off the pizza. I can truthfully admit Dwight was one man I will never forget.

    A "widower" [remarried and divorced at least once since his bereavement] sidestepped my direction question of his number of marriages by stating, "of all my wives, the one who died was my favorite." He told me he could guarantee he could entice me into marriage within three weeks.

12

Poof! Vanished without a Trace!

One guy and I accelerated from zero to sixty within a week, emailing and talking every night. Divorced, he traveled the country as a professional Wild Bill Hickok re-enactor. If his picture was accurate, he certainly looked the part. Fellow Ohioan Phoebe Ann Moses (Annie Oakley) was my hero during my tomboy years (Dusty Springfield replaced her when I was a teen-ager) so we had that in common. He promised to arrive in town, at the bus station, the night before Thanksgiving. Could I play the part of Calamity Jane (I am a klutz) to the renowned gambler and gunfighter? Would it be odd going out in public with a man stepping out of the 1800s? Would he disclose the inside story of Potato Creek Johnny? We'll never find out the answers to these and other mysteries because our last phone call the night before he was supposed to meet me was just that – our last phone call. I Never Heard from Him Again.

A tall, dark and attractive man who interested me was a lifelong resident of Annie Oakley's home town. After his divorce he moved in with his ailing, elderly mother to care for her and thus didn't have time for the three hour drive to meet me. I Never Heard from Him Again.

A younger, single stockbroker in NYC and I chatted (in the early days before I decided electronic prattle and babble was a waste of time) most evenings. Shawn had a cute smile with crooked teeth, was tall and well built, bordering on stocky, and I liked him. His co-workers made fun of him for two reasons: his favorite team was a perennial loser and he had a pet rabbit that he loved deeply. He would walk into work to taunts of "Love that Cubs' jacket!" "Hey, Shawn, how's Flopsy?"

Meanwhile, back at my own job my own love of animals made me the object of ridicule so I understood him. I thought.

Even if we hadn't lived 500 miles apart, we would not have made a romantic bond.

One evening while chatting Shawn casually mentioned he was looking at porno. Feet. Through a glory hole. ??? Don't ask me.

When he suggested he fly into town, rent a hotel, not motel, room so we could spend time together, alone, with him ... [you don't want to know], I declined. I Never Heard from Him Again.

Bruce sounded really nice, but he was too busy to meet me until fall. He was a one legged electrician who worked for himself and he needed to make all the money he could when he could. He offered to teach me his trade - next fall. I never heard from him again. I would have gladly been his apprentice. I Never Heard from

Him Again.

One of the most romantic - no, he was the very most romantic - was my Knight. We never met due to scheduling conflicts (he was Mr. Mom to his seven year old son and at the time, newly widowed, I didn't want to go out at night except to night school). His voice was velvet, and he was caring, calling me late at night, making me feel special, helping me forget my nearly unbearable pain. We didn't speak of the real world, only the one of our making. He was a complete gentleman and he captivated my imagination, and he never mentioned sex. His calls eventually stopped, and I hope it's because he's utterly fascinated and in love with a wonderful, loving woman.

One guy was my age, with red hair (my favorite), widowed, and after talking we found we had many shared interests/experiences. We both love auto racing, and guess what? We both are paralegals! We emailed back and forth one Saturday afternoon until he abruptly ended it. "Gonna watch tv." He never contacted me again. At one time, I would have emailed him, thinking I could get the party started but nope, it doesn't work that way. Men have to be the hunter and we have to be the prey. I Never Heard from Him Again.

A few weeks later I again responded to an ad. He, too, was close to my age, widowed, and employed. He even owns his own business. Two emails. That was it. When I answered his all important question of where do I live, he got back quickly. "Isn't Lancaster awfully far from Hilliard?" It's less than an hour and as a commuter and modern day circuit rider, an hour isn't a deal breaker to me. But it was to him. I Never Heard from Him Again.

A very young naive co-worker once told me that she had had a horrible night, filled with worry. When the man of her dreams didn't call her the day after a romantic interlude, their first (and as it turned out, also last), she reasoned that there could have been only one reason: he was dead! Not only are they not usually dead, they also are not kidnapped, stranded in a downed plane in a remote location, or victims of amnesia. They probably don't have laryngitis or broken fingers, either. Telephone lines go down in snow storms, and cell phone batteries go dead, but a smitten man will always find a way to contact you.

One man lives the country life, which would make a potential merger gentler. However, he spends every summer weekend at old car shows and flea markets where he is a vendor. Since he lived nearby we decided to meet. The prospect of spending hours on end with a picker who isn't Mike from the History channel doesn't ring my chimes but apparently I made an even worse impression on him. He called me within twenty-four hours of asking me out. "I can't deal with a lady preacher." Although I am an ordained and licensed minister, I do not have a church, I do not preach at or to anyone and I am no one's idea of a church, or any other type, lady. I conduct marriage ceremonies as a source of much needed additional income. I Never Heard from Him Again.

Tom and I chatted, as friends, for weeks. He told me that he throws a gallon of bleach into his old above ground pool, assuring me it is an excellent sanitizer and does not harm plastic liners, even though it is discouraged by those in the know. Since my husband departed this earth, my ancient pool has been my sole responsibility, and it was nice to have someone to advise me.

Gradually we learned little things about each other. He lives in Michigan and was recently divorced; the only time I was ever in Michigan was when my one and only husband and I eloped. He and his wife were married in 1974. My late husband and I were married in 1974. March, in fact. He and his wife were married in March 1974. The sixteenth. So were we!

You would think this little happy fest would end up in a cute romantic story, wouldn't you?

Oh, he would come down to Ohio to meet me. To have sex. For a week-end. His ex was an R.N. and he dated women with higher incomes than mine. No exceptions. He, too, petered out. (Had to use the pun.) I Never Heard from Him Again.

Jeffrey was from my hometown, and he turned out to be the younger brother of a former high school mate. That made it easy. He stopped by my office one afternoon, rang the doorbell, and stood on the stoop a co-worker peered out a side window, staring at him like he "had two heads" and not letting him inside. Joyce was shy and apparently Jeffrey was, too.

He was having a difficult enough time getting back into the dating pool, and he was not up to dealing with drama. I Never Heard from Him Again.

Randy was a good looking middle class guy, divorced three times. "Let me explain!" I did. His first marriage of twenty years ended when he was widowed. Lonely and grieving, he remarried within a few months. She was too young, he was still in mourning, and the marriage was all his fault. After their divorce, he jumped into another disastrous relationship, for the same reason, and ended up divorced again, for the same reasons. He lived in Michigan and would be coming to Columbus to attend a golf tournament. Would I care to have lunch with him? Of course!

At the time I was between cell phones so gave him my work number. MISTAKE THREE – depending upon my work phone (or anything other than a personal cell). I waited all day for his call, then received an email that night. "When I called your office I was told no one by that name worked there." Revenge of the receptionist!

Although this woman was happily married and very much the ideal wife, mother and grandmother, for some reason she was inappropriately and inordinately interested in my personal life. He didn't understand why I would give out a phone number and a fake name. I couldn't begin to explain my co-worker's action, and I Never Heard from Him Again.

Charles lived in Tennessee, so there was little chance of a romance between us. However, he was attractive (if his picture was to be believed) and friendly and fun to talk to. Then: "If we can't date, maybe you would be interested in my products. They cost a little more, but they are worth it. And if you would like to, you could become a dealer, too."

I've heard this song and dance before, almost word for word, so I politely turned him down. I don't want to be at the bottom of a pyramid. "Think it over. It's not work, because they sell themselves." He must have gone on to other prospects, because I Never Heard from Him Again.

A close friend was matched up to only one guy, a tow truck driver. A hard working man, he would be a great catch for the right woman. However, my friend has a doctorate in the law, and they would not have much in common. So a lawyer and I, just me, no fancy education, were both matched to tow truck drivers. My tow truck driver and I went out several times. Floyd, a lifelong bachelor, was a perfect gentleman, even introducing me at Tee Jays as his girlfriend before he stopped calling. A few weeks later when I ran my car off the road in the snow, I hit the cell. To my dismay even though he had lived in the same area, on the same property where he was born, his entire life (50 plus years), his business and home phone numbers were both out of service. Did Floyd find the woman of his dreams and relocate? My first thought was perhaps he died. My daughter, always the practical one, said, "Sounds like he doesn't pay his bills."

`One of my last attempts at dating began thusly: I dreamed about two white and gray feral kittens tumbling around in the yard and when I went outside that morning, there they were! I took great care with make-up and hair, then went on to work, spending the day anticipating my dinner plans.

Earlier in the week I "met" a local guy online. His name was familiar but also very common so I didn't know if he was one of my running around buddies from our teen-aged years and I didn't want to ask. It would be such a pleasant surprise to go out on a date and find out he was a true friend from my past. I always liked him but another girl was interested in him, so I kept my distance.

"Tom Jones" and I had a date at 6:00 at a Texas steakhouse. I got there 15 minutes early and waited until 6:10 before deciding I had been stood up.

I hadn't given him my phone number because I am getting more cautious. I wore my favorite black jeans - Gloria Vanderbilt (because I am madly in love with her son, Anderson Cutie - even though Gloria Vanderbilt no longer owns the brand) and a black lace blouse.

I did not care to eat by myself so I left.

I had a coupon good for one free pack of baby wipes so I stopped at the grocery and redeemed it. I didn't have the 15 cents tax on me so I had to use my debit card.

An afternoon storm caused minor flooding so I parked my car and walked home.

When I went outside to feed the ferals and Laddie, I saw three kittens playing in the yard instead of two! The third one is black and white, a little tuxedo, the same color as Laddie.

Then I noticed Laddie... He came here in 1999 and loved living outside. His health had been failing for the last year or so and I had been worried how I would get him to the vet to be euthanized because he is a huge dog. He was up walking around and eating this morning, so his death was sudden, and a blessing.

I called handyman who came out to take care of the body.

My surviving dog Eddie and I shared ice cream because I could not eat a normal supper.

P.S. I looked really nice, so my blind date was the one who missed out. I want a companion. We could go places and have fun. Maybe he could help me around the place. I don't want his money, I don't want to deal with anything other than "normal" sex, I don't want to pick up after him. I do not want to listen to him lecture about all he knows about life.

P.P.S. My date never emailed to explain why he didn't show

up. I never heard from him again but I still wonder if he was the guy in the yellow Hawaiian shirt standing in the parking lot that I waved to and walked by twice to give him a chance to approach me.

The Comedian and I had so much in common that I thought he might be The One. The first phone call lasted four hours, the second, five, the third, seven. We talked about the old days in Central Ohio: cars, local celebrities, drive-ins. He was even named after the doctor who delivered him, my dad's first cousin. At the time of our ill fated romance I was suffering from an unrelenting cold and surviving a particularly brutal winter. He lived seventy miles away, even farther in the country than I, and was also fighting the Winter Blues and Blahs. He had been a professional comedian but let his career lapse to take care of his mother.

He made me laugh, at any and every thing, and the last time he called I knew our brief courtship was coming to an end when he hung up after merely an hour and a half. I missed his last call, and was not able to return it since his number was blocked (yes, a bad sign, but he had a rational explanation as he considered himself a celebrity). He didn't like animals so we never had a chance, but I still wish we could have met.

Although in my experience, a man posting a fake picture is rare, one immediately comes to mind. Through the dating site's chat room he instant messaged me, "You are first on my compatibility list!" Although his age was stated at 49, he looked 30. Stupid me!

"Some people look younger than they actually are," was the lie I told myself. He didn't want to waste a lot of time IM'ing or emailing me, and I was a newbie, so I gave him my home phone number. I wouldn't want to let a prize like this get away. He called and we talked; mostly he talked - he has a great job at a household name manufacturing company, he drives an SUV, he lives in one of the "in" neighborhoods sixty miles away, he also rescues animals. Can you believe that? Yes, he says the right thing, and I buy it all. He would like to meet me as soon as possible. Tomorrow's Sunday, so how about it? Could he drive down to my neck of the woods, at a restaurant? Oh, no, it would be so much better if I came to his house. Could I bring my daughter and her boyfriend? I can't go to a man's house by myself. But how could we kiss with the kids around? Then, "I would like to take you to the woods where I rescue birds... You'd love it..." The next day he called me. Sorry. He can't meet me. Ever. Did his wife find out? Or his parole officer? Who knows? But this was a serious error on my part. I shouldn't have given my phone number to a man after five minutes. I shouldn't have been dazzled by his good looking picture. I shouldn't have given out so much personal information. I should have stayed aware of my surroundings even when I was in my very own home. The Internet is a portal...make sure only the harmless get through. After thinking this over, I wondered - is he a serial killer? Rapist? Both? Someone trying to see what he can get by with? Bored at home?

13

Hold Your Horses, Keep Your Power Dry, Look Before You Leap, and My Personal Favorite, Better Safe than Sorry, Men Won't Buy a Cow When the Milk is Free – Your Mother Was Right

Yes, the goal of posting your profile is to go out on dates and end up in a relationship.

However, you need to take your time. Some men can sweet talk them into your heart (and bed) and then leave you without a second thought.

They can also hurt you physically and destroy you financially.

Love at first sight, in love forever, is oh, so romantic, and it even happens once or twice in a lifetime if you're lucky, but the fastest way to lose a guy is to get involved too quickly.

Do you have standards that you absolutely insist that Mr. Right meet? No cheating! He was arrested for domestic violence but it was that bitch of an ex-wife's fault? He treats you like fine china? He's down on his luck but if you let him move in, drive your car, borrow money, he'll pay you back – with interest. He lost his job through no fault of his own, but ...

You sound desperate, darling, and desperate women often find themselves up the proverbial creek.

Burn this into your brain: until you know someone well – and you don't know someone by IMing him – you don't let him pick you up at your house. You meet at a public place. You don't give him your home address or any information that would assist him in stalking you.

Yes, it sounds hypocritical, but while you play it safe with your own personal information, you should find out his full name and place of employment.

Arrange for a friend to call you while you are on your first date. "Can I call you back later? I'm at [Restaurant] with [Date's first name]. I should be home by 11:00." During dinner you might also want to casually mention your Rottweiler, if you have one (when I began dating Sweetie was in my life but has since gone to doggie Heaven), or your son or nephew or grandson (or invisible friend), the IT engineer and self-defense instructor, insinuating brains and brawn, able to protect his loving mommy, auntie, grandmere in every way.

If your date makes unwanted sexual remarks (and they should be unwanted because they are a red flag – no man with honorable intentions would talk that way to a woman who intrigued him) or drinks too much or is rude to the server or anyone else, don't make excuses or worry about hurting his feelings. Leave.

Before getting intimately involved, and especially before introducing him to your children, moving into your home or marrying, hire a private investigator. If you feel this is over-kill, at least run an Internet search. www.whitepages.com will give you the address, phone number, age, associated people (including wife, children or other people living with him), neighbors and map.

If you would like to dig further, at the time of this writing www.peoplesmart.com offers a comprehensive background report for $39.95, including nationwide criminal check and offenses, bankruptcies, liens, and judgments, age and DOB, property and real estate records

As you know, Facebook is an easy way to check up on your guy. Just don't get hurt if he lists himself as single or there aren't a million pictures of the two of you together.

In this day and AIDS, we need to be safe. If you don't know him well enough to suggest condoms, why on earth are you considering bedding down with him? If you do broach the subject and he refuses, resist him no matter how charming he is, how lonely you are. He doesn't care about himself, let alone you.

14

Deal Breakers

After conducting a comprehensive and exhaustive in depth study, I came up with a list of deal breakers. It's not scientific, but several themes run through the personals.

Some men think tattoos cheapen a woman's appearance, especially if they are visible when she is fully clothed. However, this is easier prevented then corrected, and if you have tattoos rest easy. Other men like them, and many don't care either way.

- Except for those who request "420 times" drugs are a turn-off.
- Excessive drinking.
- Poor credit rating.
- Few or no friends.
- Beer belly.
- Poor personal hygiene.
- Dirty/messy house. Although outdoor dates are fun in warm weather and those falling in love could go on winter

hikes in January and motels abound, eventually we have to return to our own nests and share beds with our partners.

- Prison record.
- Cruelity to kids, animals.
- Poor family relationships.
- Oh, we know, we know. Excess weight.
- Drives a clunker, or even worse, doesn't drive at all.
- Out of control kids; troubled teen-agers; adult children still dependent on mommy or daddy.
- Liars.
- Thieves.
- Cheats.
- Gambling debts.
- Chronic tardiness. Some people, myself included, feel a person who is always late is selfish, self-involved and not true to his word.
- Smoking.
- Too many indoor pets. To some people, one cat, dog or goldfish is one too many.
- No pets is one of my deal breakers.
- Stingy. Closed fisted with money also equates to miserly with emotions.
- Overly emotional. Serious boyfriends (met the old fashioned way) accused me of over-reacting and being too emotional. One guy's role model was the green blooded Mr. Spock. It was swell being married to him as you can

imagine.

- Breast size. Some men think breasts are merely "fat" and others insist upon a C cup or larger. False advertising is no way to start a relationship. .Ever heard of padded bras, guys? I'm no Pam Anderson but an engineer rejected me for being too generously endowed which he believes is a sign of an I.Q. too low to be able to understand his clever conversations. To clarify, we were never intimate. He judged me by the way I look in a sweater, saying he would be embarrassed to be seen with me in public.

- Men who call women "Trouble" or "Sunshine" or "Honey." I think "Sunshine" is cute but I wouldn't want to share my pet name with 51% of the population.

- NASCAR fans. I love auto racing and don't care what anyone else thinks. The One for Me would share my enthusiasm.

- Possessiveness and jealousy – unless you find being stalked flattering.

- Gossiping is not pretty or romantic behavior.

This casual research made me realize a dental appointment is in order. I also need to pick up the house (serious understatement) and drag out the steam cleaner.

15

Remedial Dating 101

Attention, please! Before we get started on our Dating for Cougars experience, let's commit this to memory: Do not initiate contact with men. In case this isn't clear, this means do not call, do not write, do not drive by his house or place of employment in the hopes of accidentally running into him, do not email. Do not contact him under the pretext of sending him information. Do not send him forwards. In case I am not making myself clear – Do. Not. Contact. Him. First.

Burn this into your brain: Wait him out. He must contact you first.

No, it's not fair, and yes, it's infuriating, but that's the way life is!

Although I hate the idea of men being the hunters, thinking of them being pirates searching for buried treasure makes it more palpable. I'll be Johnny Depp's treasure any day!!

Now, on to dating.

Whether your husband died or divorced, it is still a death of the relationship. Perhaps you were never married; perhaps you feel you were used; perhaps your love was "from afar" or unrequited. It doesn't matter. It's over, and you are bouncing back, and ready for the best love of your life.

If you have a normal dating background, including bad relationships and sad break-ups, you have enough skepticism to keep you from being lead down the garden path. On the other hand, if you had what you describe as the perfect marriage, and your late husband is a saint, you might need to be extra careful about getting involved again. While you could be lucky the second time around, many widowed men and women have been burned. Whether they were in a rebound situation, believing the new mate would step into the deceased's shoes, or being involved with definitely the wrong person, the second marriage was an eye-opener.

♥ ▶▶

Amore!

He will treat you to dinner and a movie tonight. He's a Good Boy so you will not need pepper spray, but you could bring Parmesan cheese. What's your favorite Italian restaurant? All this, and he's single, too! ♥

If a man appears to be emotionally unavailable, he is. If he has been hurt by another woman and uses that as an excuse to not become involved with you, realize it is just that – an excuse. You of course can wait around. And wait. And wait. And when the woman he perceives as his Ms. Right appears, he will make a cannonball run toward her.

Don't eat the dust; just let him go. There really is another, better man just around the next corner, one that wants little ol' you. And the man who found someone else more - intriguing? He'll be back. That's one Rule of Life. They always come back.

Whenever my mother would make a comment about attracting men, I would ask her what she meant. Since she would never reply, I had to figure things out for myself, and I finally did learn what being mysterious meant.

We've always known that intrigue is one of romance's main ingredients, but exactly what is mystery? We won't discuss just how old I was before I realized that it isn't dressing up like Mata Hari (whatever that might be) or acting weird. It means keeping your lotions and potions under the sink and not telling every single detail of your life. That's it. "I'm sorry I missed your call. I was weeding the yard, or cleaning the refrigerator, or driving around town looking for the perfect fitting jeans because the zipper busted on my good pair because I gained weight…" is not what he wants to hear.

No, you don't give out such mundane details of your life to someone you might be interested in. See how we are using mystery here?

If you don't tell him where you were or what you were doing, he might imagine another suitor, a competitor for your affections. He will not automatically take you, and your feelings, for granted.

The more vital and alive and interesting you are, the more interested men will be in you. Keep busy with hobbies, your job - your life - and you will draw more men to you. You can't chase after love. It has to find you.

Get a Life!

If you sit behind a computer screen, chatting and IMing, perhaps dressed in sweats, how interesting or romantic can you be? If you get out and go places and see things, even if you have to go by yourself, you will have something to talk about. If you are online all the time, are you gaining weight? Are you spending all your time with a man who is online all the time? Will you ever meet or will you continue a cyber relationship? Do you want to meet? Do you want to get dressed up and go out on a real, live date? Are you afraid that real life cannot compete with Internet fantasy?

You can give Cupid a nudge, though! Working at a home improvement superstore, even part-time if you already have a job/career, will put you in the line of fire. Volunteering for Habitat for Humanity sounds good, although every guy I've seen has his lovely wife within reach. Does your community have volunteer fire fighters? What a treasure trove the firehouse could be. *Sigh.*

My romantic life consists of My Count Vronsky, otherwise known as one of the best things to ever happen to me, yet unavailable. I also went out occasionally with Fake Dead Guy, My Platonic Boyfriend (half my age, but strictly hands off) and go out on dates with any decent man who asks.

I am happier than I have ever been (with the exception of my job) even with no steady man and sporadically dating. Any type of relationship with a man with prior commitments does not count.

Think about it. My heart is light and happy. I love myself, and I also believe romance will be flying into my life soon.

The last time I heard Phil Collins singing *Two Hearts*, I got up out of my chair and danced over to the printer. My workmates didn't say anything, and might not have even noticed, since they are used to my antics, but even had I been criticized I would not care.

Working as a sample lady gave me a different viewpoint. A Pepsi dealer asked me why I was the only sample lady "under 100." I realized that where ever we go or whatever we do, or how old we get, we as women are considered men's personal flirtation devices.

WTF?

If you come from a dysfunctional family, contact him. You earn bonus points if you are The Outcast. He's no George Clooney but with a crazy name and a cape, he might make a WWF wrestler.☹

Bewitch, bedazzle, be beautiful - but never chase a man. The easiest way to lose the interest of a man is to pursue him. It took me years to learn this.

In case you need to have this pointed out again – haven't we all done these things? – emailing him to ask him a question, calling him for any reason, sending him an article you know would interest him, asking him for coffee, you just happen to have two tickets to anywhere are all instances of chasing after a man.

If you ask him out as a friend most likely he will stay a friend, and never become your boyfriend. If you cook him dinner, he might interpret that as an audition for the role of Mrs. Right.

If you need to actively involve yourself in getting a man, chase him by dressing well, having beautiful hair, looking good at all times (other than down times at home), smiling, getting involved in life itself.

If you take bewitching literally, there are many books of spells to draw love into your life. My only comments are to never get involved in the dark arts, never pay a single cent for anyone else to cast a spell for you, and never attempt to hurt another person, such as working to break up a marriage. If there really is such a force of nature, use it kindly. Burning candles to bring love into your life can be fun; black magik is just plain evil. We also must keep in mind that even white magic is considered a mortal sin by most religions.

Some women use it to develop confidence.

If you do decide to cast a spell or two, ask the universe for love, but not a particular person. If you draw someone in who doesn't want you, he will fight it the entire time you are together – in just the same way a man you go after without witchcraft. You do not want a man who does not want you. Repeat after me: I do not want anyone who does not want me.

Bewitching minus spells is creating a more beautiful life and a more beautiful you. Surround yourself with flowers when possible. Eat luscious, delicious fruit. Stay healthy and cheerful and lovely.

Dress in a feminine manner, wear flattering make-up, fix your hair. Look your best, and don't compare yourself with anyone else.

Learn to charm the pants off the man of your dreams, or anyone else. This is a lifelong project, so you will only improve as you practice, and it is a great way to ward off the scary ravages of Old Age.

To be charming, you should look and feel your best. How social do you feel in clothes that look like you've been cleaning house? How much easier is it to be outgoing and fun when you are dressed appropriately, with shiny hair and a bright smile?

Dressing to look your best does not necessarily mean expensive. Clothes that fit and flatter your figure and coloring will allow you to wear them - you don't want the clothes to wear you. Picture yourself wearing bright, light colors, soft fabrics, feminine lines. Don't you look friendly, even alluring?

Then think of a heavy, stiff, rough textured plaid suit. Isn't it cold, touch-me-not, and aging? Doesn't it scream "matronly"? Don't you feel stout and sturdy and definitely unfeminine?

Wear clothes and make-up and fragrance and hairstyles that you love so that you can be comfy in your own skin. Take care of your body, skin, hair and nails.

During a conversation, make the other person the star of the show. Ask questions. Remember important details of the other person's life. A co-worker, naturally charming, used to ask me about my newborn grandson, by name, when I was stressed out.

Don't be cloying or insincere ("You look lovely today, Mrs. Cleaver") but a genuine compliment is always welcome.

Gossip is 180 degrees opposed to the concept of charming, and makes many people uncomfortable. One man who I seriously considered being Husband #2 (and last) told me he broke up with a woman for two reasons: she asked him out first and she had the habit of gossiping.

Don't talk down to anyone, even if you are the smartest person alive.

Did we mention smile?

Arguing is not charming. I should know as I was married twenty-seven years. Unfortunately, in the day to day duels, not to mention working in a law office, I picked up the bad habit of taking the opposing view whenever anyone commented about anything. After my marriage ended so abruptly, I took stock of my life and realized that one of my worst habits was a direct result of years of my wedded bliss. In any conversation I now pick up on something, anything, to agree upon - no matter how difficult that might be - and I ignore the fighting words. Some people do seem to feel that disagreement makes for a lively conversation, and some people really do know everything about everything. Just ask them!

But we want be charming. We want people to like us. At one time that would have sounded wimpy and sappy to me. Take me as I am, or leave me. Again, that attitude departed about the same time my husband's soul left his body.

Although you can't force someone to care about you, you can make it as easy as possible.

WTF?

Only bi-sexual submissive females who are interested in bestiality need apply. No tattoos or drug use. Send full length photo to be considered. He's 63 years old. ☹

If you are divorced, please don't come across as the Bitter Half. The reason you are single is because the relationship didn't work out. Leave out the details about his toxic personality.

WTF?

She loves long distance truck drivers, and wants one of her own. She will ride along with her new BF, and flash her breasts to make everyone else jealous. His photo gets hers, if she finds him attractive enough. No country music, please. ☹

As of this writing, you can still post a profile complete with photo on several dating sites free! Email is also included in some free memberships. Since dating sites come and go, and their subscriptions vary, it is best to run a current search to see what is available. At one time, udate.com, headquartered in London, and an international site, was my favorite. Since of us need a local boy (or girl) friend, so why encourage men who live thousands and tens of thousands of miles away? Because it's fun! It's thrilling to hear a British, Welsh or Australian accent over the phone. And men from these far away countries will call you.

Also, if a man lives thousands of miles away and you aren't willing or able to relocate, you'll stay single. Although many of us say we want a boyfriend, we do encourage impossible relationships. This way - no muss, no fuss, just romance!!

Please don't cheat by using an old photo or God forbid, someone else's picture. One man was particularly upset when he found out the picture of the woman he fell in love with online was in actuality the woman's daughter, and even that picture was deceptive as the daughter had gained weight since the shoot.

I don't like getting my picture taken and always blame the camera - it's cheap - or the film - it's poorly processed, but not all of us are photogenic. After my husband died, I looked and felt a wreck so I posted an older picture. My hair was the same, but I was about forty pounds heavier. You can imagine what happened.

Many, if not most, men talked about The Three Hundred Pound Woman that haunts dating sites. She hides under a fake picture and states her weight at 140-160. She is always left at the meeting place and frequently humiliated.

Men tend to post current pictures but they have been noted to add a few inches to their height. If you're 5'3", this is not a deal breaker.

The first man I met was extremely bitter about his divorce so I offered to split a meal with him (his treat, two plates, one bill). His online picture showed auburn hair, but in person he was fully gray. He was the only man that I ever caught using an old picture and again, it wasn't crucial, but he spent our entire lunch discussing his ex. She took him for everything he had, even though she left him for another man. "I'm not one of those guys who have been divorced four or five times" so he didn't know how to obtain competent legal counsel. He never called back, so we can presume he found solace in a fellow church member.

If you never meet in person but merely chat online, even if you have cybersex - especially if you have cybersex - you are not dating. If you have cybersex before meeting, chances are you will never date. You might meet to have sex, but again, that's not dating. How can I say this? Let's just say I've known people who've had a little experience in Internet "dating." One friend ended up married, and now has a beautiful daughter, but it took kissing a lot of frogs before she married her prince.

If you use the worldwide web to find a date, don't spend a lot of time emailing or chatting. Talk on the phone going in to the relationship, and if you like what you hear, meet for a real date.

If you do indulge in cybersex, wear your prettiest lingerie, fix your hair and make-up and use your webcam. Why? If he's not drinking in your beauty (and you don't have to fully undress), he might be looking at porn or talking to another woman at the same time he is "making love" to you!

Hey! Are we this desperate? I am not, and I don't think you are, either.

A suggestion from a woman who has been disappointed by a man in Wales and another in London, and never met either one: Keep within your area code!!

It's romantic and sexy and the phone calls and accents are exciting and it's better than anything you could ever imagine, but ... it's not reality.

And although fantasy enriches our lives, we need more, at least in the long run.

Come to think of it, bring it on! Fantasy, fun, excitement, heartbreak. We've had plenty of reality in our lives, so perhaps we should enjoy this when we can. Just don't let yourself get hurt too much. (She says as she digs through her real London police badges.)

16

First Dates = Exploratory Expeditions

First dates can be like job interviews: either weeding out the poor fits, or looking for things in common. So - never argue, never get too independent and stand out. Unless he speaks extreme opinions 180 degrees opposed to your way of thinking, and he is belligerent, smile and find common ground. If he's a total freak, smile and make a graceful exit. Crazy might be fun at first, but is wearing while you are living your lives together. You might end up married to a man who spends his spare time attempting to contact space travelers. Oh, no, wait - that was my guy!!

Although the goal of a first date is to evaluate the desirability of a second, subtly is in order.

Please do not inquire or hint around about what he does for a living, what kind of car he drives or if he rents or owns. These will all be revealed to you as you get to know each other. Several men asked such personal questions, leading me to believe they are more interested in my assets than my cute ass. Yes, a man's biological urge, lust, and admiration of a woman's derrière is what I'm looking for.

Getting Ready for Your Big Date.

Arrange to meet him in a neutral place, providing your own transportation. This brings us to - clean out your car! "If you plan on meeting a man, you'd better hide the Depends, Ma." You can always depend on my daughter to point out the obvious. You probably aren't carting around bladder control pads and shampoo to be donated to a homeless shelter as I was, but a clean and clutter free car adds to the mystique of a beautiful woman.

If you have access to a beauty school, you can get a new hairstyle cheap or even free.

Always have a Plan B. Pick two or three or more pretty - and freshly washed - outfits and set them aside so that you can chose something flattering that fits your mood and is appropriate for the weather and activity of the day.

Listening to your favorite upbeat music or watching a comedy can calm nerves and lighten your mood. This is supposed to be a date, a happy social occasion, not a march to death row!

Consider a blind date an adventure, with you armed with a good attitude and locked and loaded for anything that comes your way.

Be punctual. Leaving a date standing around waiting for your Big Entrance is not cute.

Safety first. Consider getting an affordable, no contract, pay as you go disposable cell phone solely for dating to separate the wheat from the chaff. If you pick up a stalker along the way, get another cheap phone and let Mr. Weirdo Pants call the old number to his heart's content. Save any frightening text messages and hand over to the local *gendarmes*. He might earn a free ride in a Black and White (or a "bus" if he messed with Elliott Ness or any of your cities' Finest) along with an all expenses paid week-end at the Cross Bar Hotel. (This scenario is highly unlikely but it was fun thinking about since my daughter and I have both been stalked by complete strangers with no help from the Internet.)

After comfortably settled into a healthy relationship drop the gangsta phone and give Mr. Right your real number.

After cutting off service (if you didn't use a pay as you go plan) and removing your SIM card, donate to the Armed Services (www.cellphonesforsoldiers.com) or a battered women's shelter. You can also drop it off at The Shack (as insiders refer to Radio Shack) or in some cases your local library for recycling.

For safety's sake arrange to meet your date in a public place such as a restaurant or mall. While a park falls into that category, it would be too easy for you to fall victim to Stranger Danger. Regardless of how much you've chatted, emailed and talked on the phone he is still unchartered territory. Even if you ran a thorough search, you still don't know the man.

Don't allow him to pick you up, no matter how courtly that seems, and under no circumstances go to his house, even if he is a well known pillar of the community or respected member of your church.

Meet in a public place, cell phone at the ready, a friend on call, and your transportation home confirmed. Under no circumstances are you, Ms. Independent, hitching a ride home with your date. Whether your dwelling place is a nest, bungalow, cabin, chalet, cottage, duplex, ranch house, saltbox, split level, town house, apartment, condominium, flat, tenement, walk-up, penthouse, barracks, boardinghouse, dormitory, rooming house; castle, château, estate, hall, mansion, palace, villa, farmhouse, grange, hacienda, homestead, double-wide, houseboat, house trailer, hermitage, parsonage, hovel, hut, shack or shanty, you are going home alone. If romance blooms and blossoms you will have plenty of time to indulge in the horizontal mamba.

Don't overindulge in alcohol. I personally would not drink at all on a first date. Perhaps we are being paranoid, but it's not unreasonable to stay alert to the dangers of date rate (or other) drugs being slipped into your drink. Cover your drink with your hand if you turn away from it, and request a new one after you return from the ladies' room. If you don't want to appear to be suspicious of your date, merely say that the ice melted and watered down the drink.

At this writing there are two free apps for your cell phone.

Circle of 6, http://www.circleof6app.com, allows you to stay safe, prevent potential violence by connecting up to six friends or family members. Touch Circle of 6's icons twice to alert your cohorts . Circle of 6 is fast, private and user-friendly.

bSafe, https://itunes.apple.com/no/app/bsafe/id459709106, has easy to read icons including a large SOS, as well as Follow Me, I'm Here, Fake Call and bSafe Test.

Safety first; not to mention that letting tension build will guarantee fireworks the first time your stars collide.

If The Thunderbolt doesn't strike the moment you meet, give yourself a little time. Even if your date is physically repulsive, unkempt, poorly dressed and of questionable hygiene, be polite. If you feel he misrepresented himself, be cordial but cool. If he gives off dangerous vibes, excuse yourself and head for the hills.

A blind date by definition is an awkward situation. What degree of awkwardness are you willing to overlook?

Lacking in social graces (clumsy, stiff, rough hewn) can stem from shyness, a common and harmless condition. A little nervousness and modesty is attractive.

Boorish behavior, however, is a symptom of a selfish, insecure, thoughtless jerk. Rudeness to a waitress is my cue to exit stage left.

A calm, confident, cool and self-confident date could mean he is relaxed with you. If he is suave and urbane, I begin to think I'm out of my league and wonder why he asked me out and how many women he has in his stable/how many broken hearts are on his resume.

Tactless and crudeness are red flags. If your date can't get through a first date without embarrassing you with filthy, degrading and disturbing comments, make a graceful exit. Strike that. Graciousness would be wasted on him. Cast not thy pearls before swine.

Traditionally the man pays for the date. However, if you would like to impress him, add a little extra to the tip. If he wants to go dutch, or even worse, for you to pay his way, he's not interested in a serious relationship.

A young, relatively attractive homeless man recently asked me out to dinner. He subsists by selling newspapers on the street, and he was prepared to be the man and treat me like a woman.

"Thank you. There aren't that many gentlemen around."

We didn't go out, not due to his financial circumstances, but because I am much too old for him.

Growing up, teen magazines always suggested buying a concert ticket, then asking your crush to accompany you, telling him that you won them. Would you ever do this? If he is painfully shy, he could appreciate the gesture, but I wouldn't count on it. He might feel you are taking on the man's role and keep looking for the woman of his dreams.

Back to our blind date, if you are genuinely interested, compliment him, but don't gush. You aren't a stalker, so give him breathing room. If he is a nerd instead of mentioning his intellect, admire his gorgeous eyes. Hidden behind Coke bottom glasses, his baby blues probably don't get much feminine attention, and you will show your discerning nature.

If you land a nerd, you will be one lucky woman.

Maintain eye contact – but do not stare – while you are

conversing. Ask questions, nothing too personal, to make him feel comfortable. Try not to babble and please don't be guilty of sharing Too Much Information. A little nervousness is natural and can even be cute, as vulnerability is the easiest way to someone's heart.

Smile!

While on a date, be polite to everyone. If you are rude or condescending to your server, you will disappoint your date (unless he is equally rude). If your date is rude to anyone, it is bad news.

Stay upbeat. Your conniving co-worker, your disastrous ex(es), and your problems with your mother can wait for another time.

Your date is the most interesting man alive, at least tonight. Don't ask personal questions, but encourage him to discuss his life's triumphs.

Perhaps you are blessed with friendly, flirtatious humor. Tread softly, however, as jokes can backfire, inadvertently offending your date. Since your date might already be feeling insecure, your dating war stories are best saved for your friends; you don't want him to think he is just one more in a long line of near misses.

Your date doesn't want to feel he's on trial, so keep the conversation light. Ask open ended, simple questions such as "Nice restaurant. Have you been here before?"

Keep it light! No confessions, no deep dark family secrets, no apologetic explanations about your weight, no complaining about your miserable job.

If you are feeling too shy to speak, take a deep breath and speak slowly. Speak up, but if you know you are opinionated, dial it down a notch or two. Don't interrupt. Let him finish sentences before jumping in.

Braggarts are not attractive, so be yourself, remain calm and friendly and please don't try to amaze and arouse your date with tales of your awesomeness. Showing off often backfires. Make your splash subtly, with a smile.

You might be worried sick about money, arguing with your mother, stressing and PMSing, but complaining will only frighten him away. Does he need to know about your gossiping, bullying co-worker? Your ex is causing problems? No, and your date can be a Great Escape from reality, for just a few hours. Ah, romance!

Your date should walk you to your car. If he would like to get to know you better, he will hint – or ask outright – for a second date. If you are interested, you can lightly touch his arm and give him your shyest, most alluring smile.

If he doesn't ask you out, but within a day or two sends you impersonal, non-committal emails such as forwards, please don't waste your time. He might at some time grace your bed with his presence but you're not The One and nothing you can do will change his view of you.

WTF?

Contact Eric if you would like to make a quick and easy $1,000. Pic, description required. Reply with the name of your favorite continent in the subject so that he knows you can follow directions. [My favorite continent is Atlantis.] [If you are tempted by this offer, your mother should lock you in your room – no matter what your chronological age.]☹

17

Fun Dates

Volunteer – Public Service

- Walk dogs at a humane shelter.
    - If you are really ambitious, you could offer to clean cages.
    - If you aren't, perhaps you could donate bagged or canned pet food.
- Grocery shop together – great practice for your future! – and take canned goods to a food bank.
- Give flowers to people on the street or at the mall who look like they deserve a break today.
- Go through reduced racks at Walmart or other store where you can often find shirts, pants and other clothing for $1-$3. Drop off at a shelter or free store.
- Volunteer to do yard and garden work for a public park.
    - This would be particularly welcome after natural disaster such as a thunderstorm.
- Donate a few hours to Habitat for Humanity.

- Help an elderly neighbor with housekeeping chores, or deliver a hot hearty meal.

Outdoors
- Dune buggy riding.
- Although it might not be politically correct, it is fun to drive back roads with no particular place in mind. Stop and take photographs, or just keep drivin'.
- The ever popular hike and picnic (only if you know him well)
- Winter
    - Build a snowman.
    - Build a snow fort.
    - Roll around in the snow and make angels.
    - Snowball fight!
    - Go to a hockey game.
    - Sledding.
    - Hot chocolate!
    - Get a large ice block and ride it down a hill.
    - Christmas light tour.
    - Visiting a Christmas tree farm.
    - Winter hikes.
    - Chili and other stick-to-the-ribs food waiting for you in a slow cooker.

- o   Have a dinner party for two wearing costumes, eating foods and enjoying activities of a foreign culture.
- Fall
  - o   Take a drive to look at God's coloring book (otherwise known as the turning leaves).
  - o   Play in fallen leaves, either by rolling in them or throwing them around.
  - o   Carve a pumpkin – smiley face or monster, your choice.
  - o   Go for a pumpkin wall.
  - o   Find a hayride or maize.
  - o   Weiner roast and 'smores.
  - o   Hot cider and pumpkin flavored doughnuts.
  - o   Pumpkin ice cream.
- Summer
  - o   Carve a watermelon or cantaloupe.
  - o   Anything on the water – boating, swimming, fishing.
  - o   Lie on a blanket under the stars. (This is good any season.)
  - o   Water parks.
  - o   Water balloon fights.
  - o   Watch a fireworks display.

- Paddle boating.
- Explore caves. Summer is best, because the caverns are usually 54 degrees.

- Spring
  - Watch a hometown softball game.
  - Horseback riding.
  - Go shopping at a greenhouse.
  - Go for a horse drawn carriage ride.
  - After a long, harsh winter, anything outdoors.
  - Get a root beer float.
  - Feed the ducks at a local park.

Sometimes I stop at commercial growers' and walk through their hothouses to relax; no admission, just plenty of plants; not the most romantic date backdrop, but fine for a solitary pursuit. However, is there a conservatory or arboretum in your community? Walking through a beautiful landscaped public garden can be romantic and normally the cost is nominal. We have a Park of Roses and a Conservatory within driving distance.

Are you outgoing? If you are feeling silly (or creative), get out your video camera or phone and make a video, then post it on youtube. Depending on your mood, you could interview random strangers at the mall about anything that strikes your fancy from the ridiculous to serious issues of the day, at least until you get kicked out; you could also save your Academy award winning dramatization of *Streetcar Named Desire*, or just act goofy, unscripted.

Fun, cheap and sometimes silly dates (and, no, you aren't too old)
- Walk through the mall, eating Skittles or M and Ms, and speak to the first person whose shirt is the same color of the candy in your hand.
- Pick up kites at a dollar store and fly them in a park, running like the wind (or as fast as your little legs will carry you).
- Take craft paper to the park where you make and fly paper airplanes.
- Get physical at an indoor climbing gym – if you dare.
- Make boats out of aluminum foil, then float them in a stream. You could even have a regatta race.

- Is there anything more refreshing than a good old fashioned water balloon fight on a scorching hot summer's day? You could also play an informal game of water balloon volleyball, no net required.
- Go to a playground and ride the teeter-totter and swing on the swings, seeing how far up you can go.
- Blow bubbles and run through them.
- Dress up as characters in the movie you are attending.
- Draw pictures on a sidewalk with chalk.
- Get cheap balls and juggle them. Perhaps you will even have a few coins tossed at you in your new career as a street entertainer. If you can't find balls, and you've had a few too many, you could use eggs.
  - Clean up any mess you make.
- Have your palms read.
  - If you can't find a fortune teller, wear a brightly colored scarf around your head, large hoop earrings, and dramatic eye make-up and grab your date's hand.
    - Read his heart line (of course romance is in his future).
- Get your faces painted.

- Float down a lazy river in inner tubes, holding hands and singing.
- Play billiards or shoot pool.
- Take glow sticks to a lake or park and play after dark.
- Make a list of common and not so common items, then conduct a scavenger hunt at Walmart. You earn double points for things in shopping carts. Winner buys the loser a soda, sundae, or other treat.
- One root beer float, two straws, 'fifties style.
- Roller skating or blading.
- Walk or drive around town, taking digital pictures of landmarks – historic, meaningful to you, or perhaps even dives and old fashioned "beer joints."
- Brewery or vineyard tour if you dare.
- Play spin the bottle.
- Have your caricatures drawn by a street artist.

I once parked my car by the side of a road and jumped a fence to shoot several minutes of bison in action at a local park. Since it was 88 degrees with the sun straight up, the buffalo weren't doing much roaming, but I did catch them lumbering around, stopping to eat and relieve themselves. Unfortunately my date was not able to break away from work.

Would you enjoy strolling through the local zoo with your new man? It's not for everyone, though with the right guy and in the right weather you can have a blast while getting a work-out. The flamingoes are my favorite. Do you know where they get their resplendent and splendiferous – or just plain dazzling – coloring? From their diet. Shrimp! I also love the polar bears.

Most men are up for a trip to a science museum, especially involving cars and planes. Speaking of planes...

Air shows. Oh, these are fun! Watching pilots strut their stuff at a military airport makes one proud to be an American. Once when I was between dates (I am more often not between dates) I strong armed my poor daughter to a local show at a very small puddlejumper landing strip, and up into the air in a plane that had to have been 40 years old and contrary to FAA rules & regulations, in decrepit condition.

We flew around the county, but we both were terrified to look out the right window as the plane was leaning to the left, and we appeared to hit more than our share of air pockets.

We did peak out the left window. We both agreed we would have had more fun had the other passenger (it was a four seater) bathed within a day or two of the big event, but he seemed to have a great time and wasn't nearly as afraid as we were. It would have been a great date, though, just leaning into the man of my dream's strong arms as he protected me and pointed out local landmarks. The pilot/plane owner was quite good looking, too, so it wasn't a total loss.

Art museums. Gorgeous, informative, and a change of pace. Once I was lucky enough to view an exhibit of sarcophagi (stone grave containers from the time of Christ); another, Fabrege eggs.

Local Saturday night racing. Memorable moments include watching a driver so sure that he was going to win that he wasn't paying attention and hit the wall seconds before hitting the finish line (he was fine but his car destroyed), a crash whose sole injury consisted of the driver's beard catching fire, fistfights, plenty of biker types, trashy lookin' (and proud of it) women, vendor food - great fun, but definitely not for the sophisticate.

Car shows. Old car shows are the best, but they are all fun, and the admission is generally nominal or free. If you don't have a date, go with a friend or even alone. What if you met a guy there? Tooling around in a classic Corvette wouldn't be the worst thing that ever happened to you, would it?

Historic villages. It's always fun and inspiring to go back in time. If you live near a living village or farm, perhaps you could volunteer a few hours a month. You could either go on a date, or perhaps meet someone to date, there.

Graveyard tour on Halloween. In some communities, there is a hayride through a large cemetery, complete with cider and donuts. If this isn't available in your area, haunted houses are a good substitute. Again, you get scared, and he puts his strong arms around you. There are two Reconstruction era penitentiaries within driving area of my home that offer tours. Think *Shawshank Redemption*. The former West Virginia correctional facility is open to visitors most of the year, but go all out in October. I love the place, but I'm not getting into a coffin and riding down a tunnel a story or two.

Let's go to the hop, oh, baby. Any dances going on? Can you dig out a poodle skirt? How about a black leather jacket? You don't have to be eligible for *Dancin' with the Stars*, just happy to be having some fun.

Girls just want to have fun. Wear big hair, leg warmers and neon colors; dance to Springsteen; enjoy yourself at an Eighties Night. If there isn't already such an event, perhaps you could organize one at a church or other community center.

Or, take a dance class.

Miniature golf just might bring the tiger out of your date.

Any fundraiser put on by a volunteer fire department: spaghetti dinners, fish fries, dances. You're having fun, supporting a noble cause, and the firemen aren't hard on the eyes, either. Just remember to pay attention to your date!

Go-carts are young and fun.

Roller skating, ice skating - fun, cheap and good clean fun.

Is there a riding stable within driving distance? Once on a double date with my then husband and our son and his bride, we rented horses for an hour ride. I was terrified, determined to back out, until the owner's seven year old granddaughter gave me a little talk, and the oldest, most gentle horse was brought out for me. The horses knew the way, and although I'd never ridden before, when we went down a hill, I automatically stood up and kept my balance.

My husband [aka as Lorne Greene that particular day] rode a stallion, and led the way. The funniest part was that I suspected that this was Bill's first time on a horse (or if not, no more than his second or third), yet he rode high in the saddle. My poor son rode behind me and ahead of his wife and obviously felt responsible for both our safetys, mostly his scatter brained, silly mommy. This is something I would like to do again, and am keeping for Mr. Right.

Another thing I am saving for Mr. Right (and maybe even for Wedding #2) is a hot air balloon ride. I'm going to dress all up in a white eyelet gown, with fresh flowers in my hair, the embodiment of femininity and romance.

County fairs. Stealing a kiss on the ferris wheel, riding the carousel, visiting the 4H barns, being a teen-ager again. I met a beau years ago at our local county fair when a guy who was interested in me dragged me down the midway with a cane, then threw me in a sow pen. His friend pulled me out - oh! was I afraid the sow would stomp me to death, protecting her piglets - and he and I dated casually for several years.

Here in the midwest we have Corn Mazes, which are exactly what they sound like: a puzzling path cut through a corn field.

Some commercial farms also have hay mazes in their barns. You crawl through tunnels of stacked hay or straw. Please keep in mind these are made for average people so if you are queen size, or if you suffer from claustrophobia, you might not enjoy the pursuit.

Weiner roast. You can always grab hot dogs, buns, and charcoal plus lighter, then relax at a park if you don't want to have it at home.

If you belong to an organization such as a church, you could suggest an 80s night, weiner roast, hayride.

Is there a train ride in your area? Some areas have Halloween and Holiday train rides, as well as scenic, seasonal tours.

18

Bad Dates (Or, More Kindly Put, We Weren't Right for Each Other)

My first date was with a guy who had auburn hair (a favorite) in his online picture. When I entered the restaurant - The Tower, a restaurant/bar that has been in existence with one name or another for 100 years - I noticed a man "hiding" behind the door. Greg! With completely gray hair! That was fine with me, because my photo wasn't recent, either. When I saw the prices, I suggested we share one meal on two plates.

His story: his wife of twenty-five years took up with a fellow church member and sued him for divorce. "Not one of those guys who's been married and divorced four or five times and knows all the tricks", he lost everything he had. He would have taken his ex back after her affair but she wanted the new guy. He has child support, house payments (the Mrs. didn't work "outside the home" - and in my world if you don't work "outside the home" once your kids are old enough for you to go out and slay the dragons along with your husband you don't work - period) and college expenses.

I would have gone out with him again but he didn't ask me. I liked him, but I think it was too early for both of us. Also, I was so green at this point in my life I didn't realize his passing on a romance with me was truly a gift from the gods. He had to leave his church due to the divorce but I can only assume he met a wonderful woman at his new church and they are happy.

A Great Guy, but Our Timing was Off. On sunny and warm days when I'm stuck on my desk, I occasionally think of Bob and think of what might have been. He was tall and thin, my age, intelligent. I liked him at first sight! Wearing jeans and jacket and boots, he was my ideal cowboy, yet urban, and urbane. We met at a butterfly exhibit at the conservatory. It was my idea and he even paid admission. As you can imagine, it was a relaxing afternoon. Or, it would have been, had he not been so defensive. Divorcing after thirty years of marriage, he was looking for an argument, and I was still a widow struggling through the devastation of the end of my own way of life. I wanted security.

After walking through the exhibit, we sat and talked, he with his feet up on a table, his chair tipped back.

"We're equals, and that's what you women want, so you can pay for the root beer."

I did. It was ice cold, in a bottle. "All men just want to control things, right?" and "You women have all the answers" peppered the conversation.

He took early retirement, withdrew all the money, and

bought land down in the hills. He was committed, and it was too late to back out. He was building a house with his own hands, and sleeping under the stars. If he couldn't find a woman to join him and help with finances, he'd get a job at the big box store. There were several obstacles. I cannot retire, and there are few jobs within driving distance of his new home. I have my own place, and my own life. I don't want to relocate. He was obviously on the rebound, and even though he couldn't understand it, I am nothing like his wife!

Would I have had a romantic interlude with him? You betcha! Did he ask? No.

What's he doing now? Is he with a woman who loves him? Does he make her happy?

Did he get his house finished? I picture a cathedral ceilinged cabin with hardwood floors and minimal furniture, fireplaces in the great room and loft bedroom and a wraparound deck. A smooth stovetop and quiet running dishwasher, both black, with a stainless steel refrigerator create an efficient kitchen. Am I crazy? Here I am living in a run-down ranch and he's living in a chalet. He's had time to mellow, and he and his new bride are living happily ever after. And I'm still alone, cuddled with my dogs, relaxing after a hard day at same old job, watching Kathy Griffin on the old squawk box and knocking back a diet grape soda.

Why couldn't I have seen it then? A big hug and kiss could have knocked that chip off his shoulder. It might have been fun snuggling up in his sleeping bag. Maybe he would have taught me the fine points of hammer and nails. Maybe I just don't understand men.

He might not understand women, either, because it takes a special type of gal to do without a bathroom while her man builds the house of his dreams. And, yes, he gave the impression that it was all about him and his wants and his desires and his needs and the woman would be merely his accessory. Instead of my long-time dead end job where I at least am able to walk around the city on my lunch hour and sit down while I work, I might be employed at the same big box store he contemplated as his own last resort. Perhaps I should be thanking my lucky stars (I actually thank God for everything in my life) that I am still single.

WTF?

Flirtin' ain't hurtin' and eatin' ain't cheatin'. ☹

I really thought Phil could be The One. He was an engineer (I require a man with a decent job or at least be employed), divorced, and lived in a nearby town. He didn't waste months, weeks, or even days chatting/emailing before asking me out. He even agreed to drive to the Olive Garden in my town.

He showed up bearing gifts: a bouquet of roses and a bottle of wine.

Available, intelligent, employed, and romantic!! What else could a girl want?

Our entire evening went thusly:

There is something you need to know. I am in love with Margie. I have been in love with her since second grade, and I will always love her.

Even after she moved away in the sixth grade and Phil never saw her again, she was still the love of his life.

No, I don't know what she looks like. Since he hasn't seen her since pre-puberty, I doubt he could describe her, either.

His wife didn't understand, or appreciate, this Great Love.

After the divorce, the first thing he did was - you guessed it, didn't you? On to the Internet, where he searched until he found Margie.

She's married. She's a pastor. She has her own church in Minnesota.

Phil's first email was answered with a matter of fact "I'm married." The second response was from her husband.

The third was from the police department of her home town.

Didn't the fact that the police department contacted him mean that she was interested in him? Didn't that indicate that she indeed wanted to hear from him? Why couldn't he call her? She had to have loved having the altar of her church filled with roses, didn't she? Why was it fair that she could talk to the police about him but he couldn't contact her? Why can't he donate flowers to her church?

After dinner, I got into my car, calmly so as not to agitate him, roses and wine in my arms, and locked my door, immediately.

Phil followed me, pulled up beside me at a traffic light, and gave me a moon-struck look. I punched that Cougar through five speeds, racing several exits past the road leading to my house, then made a u-turn, and drove to the State Patrol Station, pulled in and parked for a few minutes. That's why God made staties! My date - who, astonishingly, looked and acted perfectly "normal" - called my house before I got home, but fortunately my daughter told him I had run off and she didn't know where I was or if I would ever come home.

I gave the roses to my elderly spinster neighbor who due to family responsibilities never had the fabulous opportunities for romance that have blessed my life (as you can see by my dating history), and the wine to my mother, a lifelong teetotaler until her later years when she had a glass of the grape before hitting the hay.

We met at a pizza restaurant, and Kenny was generous. "Order whatever you want," he said, waving his ex-wife's debit card. Oh, it was fine with her. She's a doctor and has plenty of money, and he lives in her basement, taking care of their kids. Well, the arrangement did work well, up until the time he wrote a letter to "foreign" neighbors, tied it to a rock and threw it through their living room window. Rockets' red glare, bombs bursting in air! I could almost hear a post September 11 Toby Keith song playing in the background. He'll send them to hell if he gets the chance. Due to the restraining order, Kenny has to find a new place to stay, and soon. He's a very cheerful man. Surely you didn't think he was one of those crazy anti-social loners, did you? He's a restaurant manager by trade, and if you ever went to his old job, you could see the waitresses, half of whom he "hosed," which is why he is divorced and unemployed. One woman he met online was not attractive enough for him (yes, according to him she was "fat" – and he was no John Stamos, either), but he did "give himself" to her, leaving as soon as the deed was done. When she offered him a freezer full of beef as he was gliding out the door, Kenny slowed down long enough to take with him what he could carry in both hands, telling her he would be back for the rest. No, he never went back. I almost liked him. In his own way he was personable, which is more than could be said of some.

One guy chatted me, then asked me for lunch. When the men are local, it makes sense to meet them early on, instead of chatting. If the chemistry is there, why wait and if it isn't, you haven't wasted time. He was tall, athletically built, intelligent, gainfully employed, and regimented: lunch or dinner, with a mandatory good-bye kiss. No kiss, no second date. We went to a yuppie restaurant, talked, enjoyed our meal, and when we parted, I hesitated. We were in front of my office and one co-worker lives her life like my former mother-in-law, with her nose out the window, watching, watching, watching - everything. How can you give a man a quick kiss with an audience? He also had a "rule" that after he begins dating, chatting sessions start with "I love you." Perhaps no one has ever loved me, or perhaps the men I met were honest, but no one has ever come home, logged on, and flashed "I love you." In this man's world, the woman automatically responds with "I love you" before they continue their conversation. Also, why instant message or chat a person who lives within driving distance? Why not talk on the phone, or better yet, see each other in person??? As in, in the flesh???? This can lead to interesting evenings as in flesh to flesh romance. He also attended riverfront concerts every summer, every Friday night, no matter who he was dating. However, the pork roast, mashed potatoes with skins and creamy cole slaw at the restaurant were simply marvelous, darling. And he would be a good husband to the right woman. My married life was chaotic at times, and living with a ramblin' man brought out the butterfly in me. Keep things light, pizza for Christmas Eve dinner, Easter egg fights with the kids, an occasional water balloon welcome home, nothing is written in stone and let's not get old before our time. How about a concert one Friday night and a peace rally (or any cause close to your heart) another? Or even staying home and watching Comedy Central?

Meeting one man for lunch, I thought I looked romantic and feminine wearing a black velvet dress with red roses and a matching fabric rose in my hair. It must not have stirred his soul because he immediately went into business mode. After ordering chicken wings (not my favorite) with celery sticks (yuck), he conducted an interview. He owned a marketing company and when he learned that as a volunteer I created and maintain a very low tech website for an animal rescue organization, he went into high gear, questioning my methods and training. Everything I do is wrong! Our group consists of a few Christian women who work very hard to raise funds to pay medical expenses for homeless animals and place them in loving homes. We don't have money to pay a professional, and we feel we do a good job. But my date made sure I realized that he is a professional and I a rank amateur. (This was not news.) I took the walk of shame leaving the restaurant, because not only did we not make a love connection, but I also failed an imaginary job interview. With his take-charge personality he most likely is a success at the love game. However, I don't like games, and I don't play 'em.

WTF?

Straight guy will get the chicks; wingman provides camera and place. Girls are encouraged to apply for this modeling opportunity. He will help put together a portfolio that he will submit to his contacts in NYC, Veg-ass, and City of Angels. [If you believe any of this, your mother should lock you in your room.]☹

Daffodils and lilies, coloring eggs, chocolate bunnies, tinted coconut nests, baked ham, Panoramic Sugar Easter Eggs, peeps, jelly beans, bonnets, little boys in big boy Sunday Go to Meetin' suits, ribbons and ruffles, pastel dresses, baby chicks, patent leather shoes --- and a date with grifter. These are my Easter memories. Eugene was a mountebank of the first order. Not merely a rascal, he must have spent his entire life refining his ability to swindle to a fine art.

On our first (and last) date I - an admitted poor widow - was thisclose to buying him a used Corvette, the car of my dreams that will mostly likely remain a fantasy. Since you know how careful (paranoid to the point of not letting another man into my life) and how I preach about watching for warning signs, you might get a giggle about my day before Easter "tail."

Eugene said he wasn't good with the computer, so instead of emailing, could he just call and make a date?

Ten points for him!

He offered to pick me up but instead we arranged to meet at

a quaint village near my house. Population 600, the village's main thoroughfare consists of three blocks of antique shops and one small tavern-pizzeria.

The day of our big date, the bar was filled with bikers, but Eugene was able to sweet-talk the waitress into giving us our own table. Tall and thin, with a smoker's cough, he tapped his pocket. "Anything you want, Darlin'..."

He didn't eat a bite of pizza. "Stomach problems, Darlin'." Not wanting to look like a pig, I ate only two pieces and quite reluctantly left the rest.

He was a VietNam veteran (oddly, I've met men who if they indeed had had a tour of duty in Southeast Asia would have been toddlers if not an ovum waiting to be fertilized sometime in the future but he was in the proper age range) and an entrepreneur. He never had the benefit of a formal education, and he didn't need one.

We walked down the brick sidewalk, to an art gallery housed in a late 1800's two story home. He introduced himself to the recent art school graduate-gallery owner and by the time we'd meandered up the stairs, through the three rooms, and came back down, he had a verbal contract for a vinyl computer generated banner that he insisted was necessary to market this new business.

Only a smooth operator could convince an artiste to buy something so visually discordant.

"Are you creating the sign yourself?" No, as you recall he "is not good on the computer."

He'd pay $1,000 to have it made, and charge him $2,000. "See how easy that was?"

We drove his Cadillac, not new, but not old, either, up the road to a large car dealership.

I confessed that I, too, would like to be my own boss. This was not the brightest statement I've ever made.

His cell phone rang every ten minutes or so. Fingers over his lips, he would mouth "Daughter... gotta take this call."

"Yes, Honey, I'll be home soon." He explained that his daughter was excited about the next day's Easter dinner, including her mother (his ex-wife).

Back to the scam, I mean, our date. "I have a t-shirt printing business. I take it to fairs. Comes with printer, supplies and trailer." He was tired of it, and he was willing to sell it to me for $10,000.

I actually considered this! No more sitting in an office during sunny weather. No more bosses. Where would I come up with $10K? Please! Don't confuse me with the facts. Details, details. How unromantic.

He drove to the used Corvette section, and when a salesman came over he said he wanted to test drive one costing – you guessed it - $10,000.00. Cash.

He smiled at me.

And that's how I rode in a Cadillac and a Corvette, both in the same day, and still escaped the charms (and arms) of a midwestern scalawag.

P.S. I never heard from him again.

Reminder: Perhaps an embittered aunt cautioned you that men "are only after one thing." She might have been right! However, the thing some of the men are after is money, not your pure heart or juicy body.

I didn't want to go out with the John Edwards lookalike, but he insisted. Kevin's profile picture showed a 50ish handsome man wearing a blue (the universally flattering color) shirt and white sailing pants. I told him that he was too attractive for me, and after several of the previous fiascos of men rudely rejecting me, I wasn't up for more.

We met at a spaghetti place, and he looked just like his picture. Kevin was polite and happy to meet me. He put me at ease.

He was a pleasant conversationalist.

After his third wife torched their condo in a fit of drunken rage, he moved back to Ohio and in with his mother. He was currently delivering pizzas, but his fortunes were going to improve. Dramatically. What would I think about dating a guy who is going to be worth $29,000,000.00 (yes, you read that right - million) over the course of ten years? He did have a business partner, so it would really be half of $29,000,000.00, but that would still make a good living, wouldn't it?

The thing was, he and his partner invented a part that was vital to a certain industry, and they held the patent. It was a guarantee of the good life, at least for the ten years of the pay-out.

He also thanked me for fixing myself up because the last woman he met over the Internet showed up with (unfashionably) ripped pants and dirty hair.

He walked me to the car, opened the door for me and said he enjoyed our dinner, and it was well worth the money. (I'm a cheap date and always offer to pay my own way.)

He was charming, handsome, and not after anything. I told him I was not comfortable with someone that well-to-do or good looking. We could have been a couple had I not been so insecure and suspicious. And, yes, I was just being polite about his earning potential, but I was sincere about his looks intimidating me.

One memorable date stared at me as if I were an insect while I ate steamed mussels. He brought along a picture of him wearing swim trunks – but skinny is nothing to brag about – as well as photos of his house and his cats. And, most importantly, his mother. I loved my mother very much, but I would never show her picture to a blind date, prompting, "Isn't she an attractive woman?" He carried all his pix in a ziplock bag. We can only hope he never loses it!

He also told me about his former girlfriend's menstrual difficulties. As she avoided having sex with him, it could only be "female troubles." Any woman would be thrilled and honored to be with a charmer like him, right? Although he'd passed his fiftieth birthday and he longed to marry, he'd never met a woman to compare with Mom.

Stopping at the grocery on the way home I enjoyed the smiles from a man who was younger and better looking than the man who treated me like I was the most unattractive woman who ever lived. Too bad he was married. (We can only assume the woman and children surrounding him were his.)

Last New Year's Day, while driving to Walmart - gotta get those after Christmas clearance bargains as well as the generic cold & sinus medicines - I received a phone call. Since I had spent the morning cleaning and watching *CSI Miami*, and although I did clean up, my ill-fitting jeans and in need of a fresh shampoo hair were not up to meeting a new guy.

So, I asked if we could meet at 3:00, in my neighborhood.

I washed and conditioned my hair, borrowing my daughter's expensive stuff. Then I ripped through my closet trying to find a black velvet blouse with ruffles and velvet handkerchief hemmed skirt. I never did find it, and the new dress I got on clearance at KMart for $2 flattened my bosom, so I couldn't wear that. (I later offered the dress on craigslist's free section which a young English Second Language speaking man picked up at my workplace, causing hilarious gossip.) So I settled on - I can't even remember! Oh, yeah, the black velvet dress that I wore to my husband's funeral. I donned black patterned tights (Dollar Tree) and high black vinyl boots ($3, Walmart clearance), topping it off with the gorgeous pink leather coat Santa brought me for Christmas. I did the best I could, considering I'm "over thirty" and a "few pounds" over my fighting weight.

He was short, stocky, and pathetically nice. His wife of thirty-five years died two years previously, leaving him a big surprise. Since she had been signing ("forging" apparently was too strong a word for the gentleman to utter) his name on loans all their married life, he doesn't own title to his house, and her life insurance was gone. He consolidated several loans and is paying off her debts. When I told him about a friend who shocked her husband with $20K of debts (with nothing to show for it), he said he wished it would have been $20,000. He will be paying off the debts, as well as working two full-time jobs, the rest of his life, but he is an honorable man.

He couldn't afford to buy a meal and I wouldn't have let him pay, anyway, so we went to the food court at the mall and each had a Coca Cola. I have had only two regular (sugary) Cokes in awhile (the other, when I was in the hospital with shingles & there wasn't a Zero to be found), but what the hay! Let's splurge.

Maybe my "date" would have looked better to me if I hadn't spent the morning watching a David Caruso marathon, but you never know.

He is a nice guy trapped in a miserable situation not of his making, and I can't wave my magic wand to make his debts disappear.

I waited a few months before accepting another date, mostly because that guy was so pathetic: financial problems, no women interested in him, etc.

However, once again I thought time's awastin' and I'm not getting any younger, and I don't want to be alone the rest of my life. So -- I went out with a guy who seemed nice, and I thought it would be good to get out and enjoy life.

He was nice, very nice. He also is not only unemployed (he lost his job of twenty-six years when the plant closed - and I felt bad about that because it's happened to many people, including me), but trying to get disability. He feels if he takes a job he will ruin any chances of getting Social Security Disability, so he hasn't had any income in close to three years. He lives with (and off) his 80 something parents. Although he wanted to buy me dinner, I insisted I wasn't hungry (a lie, as I am always up to enjoying a good meal) and suggested we share a hamburger and fries.

When he told me he is taking care of them more and more I said that was wonderful, and my parents are "gone." My date: Where did they go? Do you know where they are?

Me: They are DEAD.

He would like my daughter to be friends with his daughter because they are the same age, and his daughter needs a friend because her ex-husband took the kids and she doesn't know where they are. I told him my daughter doesn't have any time right now. (My daughter doesn't have kids, but we would like to think if she did, she would know their exact locations at all times.)

We could go on and on and on with this little story, but I kept thinking I needed to stop and buy a pair of tweezers on the way home and kept wishing I could be home watching youtube, thinking of Clay Aiken singing *Everlasting Love*.

So on the way home I did stop to buy tweezers and I walked through the store singing *Everlasting Love* out loud. My singing voice is not good. I didn't care.

One of the worst dates I ever had went thusly: me in my Miss Monroe fake fur, clingy red dress, full make-up. He: casual, cotton clothing, almost hippie in appearance.

I ordered: a sugary cola and French onion soup.

He: salad and tea.

After this disaster, he wrote me a three page letter suggesting liposuction on my neck and stomach, plastic surgery on my face, especially my hose. I also need a good dentist, should dress more appropriately and eat healthier. Otherwise, not only would he not want me, but neither would anyone else. This man was intelligent, sensitive, and fun. He was also short. Did I comment on that? Would it have mattered to me? No. Why did he send me the letter? Wasn't it obvious? He wanted to help me and perhaps I didn't realize that my neck needs work, and that my stomach protrudes.

However, he loves my hair.

Oh, yeah, I later found out he was married (for the second time), to boot!

Ahmed was a 28 year old visitor to the Land of Liberty and I was – old enough to be his mother. A virgin, he hoped I could give him dating tips. He picked me up at work for lunch. We walked to a local art show, then to Wendy's where we went Dutch. He was polite and ever the gentleman. He'd been promised to a girl in his homeland since infancy, but after attending college in the States, he decided to stay. He was a computer professional and proudly showed me pictures of his dream machine, a flashy Mustang. At no time did he touch me.

He walked me back to work, going into the building giving Ms. Gossip more twigs and logs for her bon fire.

My "date" with someone "a year older than her son!" was the sole topic of conversation, mostly one-way, with anyone brave or naïve enough to walk into her radar.

That night he emailed me: my glossy lips, my toned lower body (I was wearing a coat when we went out so my midsection was mercifully hidden)were all he could think of.

Being a practical man, he then logged off to watch a porn video.

The last I heard he hooked up with a single mother of two who used him for sex, then dumped him.

Wilbur told me he is a driver, which in my addled brain translates as race car athlete, not delivery man. However, after coming back to reality, I was eager to meet him and he appeared to be equally enthusiastic, because he called me between stops the entire week before our Saturday night date. Divorcing after fifteen years of marriage, and very shy, he was bringing along his seventeen year old step-son. I was welcome to bring my family, too, but they were unable to accompany me. Oh, ok, they didn't want to go.

We met at a family restaurant at an upscale mall and he generously paid for my dinner (anything I wanted). He sat next to his step-son, and across from me. He looked at the seventeen year old the entire time and the boy held up their end of the conversation.

Wilbur was tall and thin, a decent hard-working family man and a definite catch for the right woman. I would have liked to have had the opportunity to get to know him better, but I never heard from him again after his terse reply to my thank you for dinner email.

Another man drove up from the Ohio River to meet me, bringing me a trash bag of white socks. He digs ditches for a living so he needs a new pair every day, and since he buys them in bulk he decided to share with me. He was very nice, but when he told me that every woman he was ever with cheated on him, with his coworkers, it scared me off.

William sent me pictures of his brick house (much nicer than anything I've ever lived in), but not himself. A tall, nerdy guy, he and his two daughters were passing through town on their way to Tenneessee so the girls could spend the summer with their grandparents. We met at Pizza Hut. William had been widowed and divorced and needed a mother for his seven year old. It was not interested in me, so I talked with his kids. His teen-aged daughter taunted him by reminding William that her bank account financed the trip. Even though he was a generation or two too young, as am I, he thought good rock music was Buddy Holly. (It is, but he doesn't seem to realize there is much more to enjoy.) In a way, he resembled Buddy Holly, except he was still alive. It must have been the glasses. The teen-aged daughter amused me. I've raised two kids so not much intimates me. I liked the little girl and hope William found someone to love and protect her.

Want to hear about Fake Dead Guy, my Platonic Boyfriend? We met in one of those cute ways. I was leaving flowers at a cyber cemetery when I saw a tribute to a guy my kids' age, buried in the local city cemetery. Fake Dead Guy was said to be a tortured artist who died on All Hallows' Eve. His picture looked familiar. It made me feel sad, especially since his last name was that of a former co-worker, so I left a message in his memory.

Several months later I received an email stating, "good news! I'm not dead." We started a correspondence, and since my daughter was temporarily out of state, my son is always busy with his family, I was lonely, and we were both a little zany, we decided to meet. We live about six miles apart.

Our first date, if you want to call it that, we met at the mall and had an all you can eat brunch. Well, I had all I could eat, and I guess you could say he had all he could eat, too, except that he has a bad stomach and he can't eat much.

We talked as if we had known each other forever, and then walked around the mall until he said he needed to sit down. "Don't you ever get tired?" (This from a 28 year old man, but I've heard it from other men, too.)

"How do you walk in those things?" My pointed toe red high heel boots (clearance, $3.00) aren't exactly comfortable but they aren't killers, either. And they are flattering.

I couldn't tell how the date went, because I never can, but obviously he liked me as there was a long email awaiting me by the time I arrived home. (After a date I normally stop at a store and walk around as a cooling off period.)

He felt funny about it, but he thinks we have so much in common - we do! - and how can he find a woman my age attractive? But he does.

Fake Dead Guy is cute, but a little ... bloodless... reminiscent of a young Christopher Walken.

Once he took me to the local diner, his favorite place of all, where he everyone does know his name, and when we ordered our meal, he took it for granted that I would also order a mushroom burger (I love mushrooms!) but was dismayed when I asked for mustard? Mustard? He hates mustard! So did my late, great, equally nutty husband. But I love it!

When my daughter came home to stay, Fake Dead Guy, My Platonic Boyfriend invited her to dinner with us. Even though he is two months older than she, and she is very attractive, he was nice to her, but he did not show any interest in dating her.

We've had plans to go ghost hunting, but something has always come up and one of us (him!) has had to cancel. He knows some weird haunted and secluded cemeteries (of course he does!) in the southern part of the state.

Oddly enough, both of us went to cemeteries with our dads when we were growing up, although my dad (a God fearing man) took me only to honor our ancestors, not stir up anything.

Our main date so far was hiking. He picked me up and we drove to a metro park that has a three mile trail, first stopping at a deli (where this time everyone knows my name) for picnic supplies. "Oh, is this your son?" "No," I told the embarrassed deli friend, laughing. "This is my date!"

We took our hike, then came back and had lunch. He told me his dreams and I told him mine. He is a poet (quite talented, from what I've read) and he thought he would have been a famous rock star by now. "Don't give up. Never give up."

For our next date, we were going to hike up our local mountain, a sandstone reminder of The Glacier that local historians talk about, endlessly it seems. However, after waiting for half an hour, my limit, and not seeing him, I went home. Nope, I didn't call him. I don't call men.

He emailed me later. He is a jerk! He is so sorry! He overslept! Why didn't I call him?

Later he asked me to spend his birthday with him because he doesn't want to be alone. We are going to a restaurant and he will pay. Even though he has little money (maybe even less than I do if that is possible), and he never "tries anything", he always picks up the check.

His latest: he can't get his mind off another woman. Oh, there's no reason to be jealous, and it just reinforces my feeling that he likes older women...much older women...

This particular gal who caught his eye has been dead for many years. He found her picture in a genealogy search and all he knows about her is that she never married. I suggest that perhaps they were in love in a previous life. He can't find out where she is buried, and he very much wants to visit her grave, so I'm making a trip to the library to review graveyard records.

I have to admit that from her picture, she is a very nice looking woman, especially since she isn't wearing make-up. You would think he would have prefaced his statement of interest in a long dead woman by saying, "I know this sounds crazy..." or "Don't laugh, but..." but he didn't. Just "I can't get this woman out of my mind..."

So - I exercise, and I'm friendly and loving and caring, and I have two men interested in me, one of whom wants to have sex with me (if only he didn't have to worry about that pesky marriage thing) and the other - talks about dead people.

After several years of on and off friendship, dancing around a relationship or whatever is going on, he continues to text me. I admit I like him, but don't know what to do with him.

19

Dating Tips for Older Women

We older women have life experience, independence and maturity that many men find attractive. We don't need to compete with younger women.

Many people suggest that a woman over 45 dress her age instead of making a fool of herself by adorning herself with clothing more appropriate for her daughter or niece. Dressing younger seems to run in the family; while all the other mothers wore pantsuits mine was in heels, pink frocks and light lipstick. If you need to be concerned about anything, choose clothing that is appropriate for your body type. (And dress a little younger than your actual age – you're in the dating pool, not getting ready for a retirement home.)

However, acting your age is highly recommended. Pictures of you hugging a toilet or chugging a brew will not win you a date with Mr. Right. A genuine smile and the ability to pay attention and listen to your date is much more attractive. Don't you agree?

If your date is younger, please resist the urge to mother (smother) him. However, this is not written in stone. One friend who received very little nurturing from his own mother is married to a childless woman twenty years his senior. . You might say Janet is the ideal mom because although she babies Matt, she never nags him What if Matt grows up someday and wants to leave his "mother?" What if? The relationship appears to be working now, and today is all we have.

If you are on your second (or third or fourth) time around, your priorities might have changed. Whereas an eighteen year old might go for a good looking playmate, an older (and wiser – we hope) woman probably would care more about a man's dependability, honesty, and willingness and ability to provide for her.

While a grown up Pollyanna is not most men's fantasy woman, a positive outlook is refreshing. Count your blessings. Be grateful. Smile!

If you are interested in a younger man, and I mean much younger, don't be embarrassed. We won't get into the whole "when a man dates someone 30 years younger it's ok, but when a woman does it..." debate, because who cares? Joan Collins married a guy at least thirty years younger, and she seems to be doing well at the moment. Gina Lollabrigida, at seventy-nine, married a man thirty-four years younger, after dating him for twenty-two years. If you are attracted to a younger guy, and more importantly, if he is attracted to you (he's after your ass, not your assets), enjoy yourself! If this language – making sure he is after your ass, not your assets – offends you, that is good! This means you will remember the statement and perhaps take it to heart. If you have lived a sheltered life, you need to know that some men do take advantage of innocent women. Whatever your financial situation, you don't need to fund a man's lifestyle. This said, enjoy yourself! If it doesn't last forever, what does?

If you have been chatting, emailing and talking over the phone to someone intriguing, arrange a meeting in a public place within a week or two. Otherwise, you are setting yourself up for disappointment and possible heartbreak by building up an imaginary romance in your mind. I confess I learned this from bitter experience. Also, The One might be in reality Mr. Keyboard Romeo with only God knows how many online flirtations going.

Dress feminine and flirty, not slutty, in clothing that flatters your body without being too revealing.

Have fun! Ask him about his interests, favorite sports teams, cherished cars, popular pursuits, pet projects, adventures and (funny) misadventures, and physical exercise, if any. Tae kwon do, anyone? Or does he spend an occasional Lazy Day? How about he celebrates holidays? Does he prefer family get-togethers or does he head for a cabin in the wilderness?

At the end of the date, you should know whether or not you would like to see him again. If he clearly is more interested in you than you are in him, and he doesn't appear to be a stalker or other dangerous type, would you consider a second date? Or will you gently let him down? You can always wait a day or two and tell him that a former flame came back into your life and you want to see if the relationship works out this time.

What if he isn't attracted to you? It hurts, of course it does. But if he doesn't want you, you truly don't want him. You are wasting your time and could overlook the entrance of Mr. Right while hanging onto a one-sided amour. Take it from *moi*, possessor of way much personal experience in this area.

20

Ads I Have Posted

Here is my latest - and last (famous last words) - ad.

"Sense of Adventure? Today I went on a hike at a metro park. Yes, it was 25 degrees out, and it was way too cold, but it was a great way to spend a Sunday afternoon. It would have been even better with a special guy."

Responses included one from a guy who told me he was "well endowed" (because as we all know, women actually want to hear that kind of romantic talk from strange – in more ways than one - men) and he would keep me busy inside instead of outdoors; a welder who sent his picture, minus his shirt and sporting a grizzly gray beard down his chest; someone who insisted that I claimed I went "biking" yesterday and refused to believe that I never learned to ride a bike due to my over-protective mother; a man who looks old enough to be my father; a man who was out the door to hunt deer... Which one should I chose?

This was one of my favorite ads:

"Cherry Bomb" was my teen-aged life [no Carly Simon or James Taylor fan, but John Cougar – I know he stopped using the middle name but I love it – Mellencamp was a Midwesterner growing up the same time and apparently the same way as *moi*]. Recently I was remembering my innocent teen-aged years and wished I could drive around town with a cute guy, laughing and having fun and maybe even stop at a lake and fool around a little. That's not even possible today because a woman has to be so careful. Many guys in my age group like James Taylor but I was never a fan. Have a good evening, All!"

P.S. By mentioning my innocent teen-aged years, I thought I would make it clear that I'm a down to earth woman looking for a nice, uncomplicated guy.

Responses included a seventeen year old, several married men looking for erotic (and more sexually adventurous escapades) times, one who said I sounded nuts (yet sent his picture), along with the same ones who respond to every ad: a stubborn divorced guy who refuses to drive anywhere or spend any money on a date (yet writes an encyclopedia in his introductory emails) and an equally stubborn widower who promises to take a woman anywhere she wants, treat her like a queen, and do whatever makes her happy yet insists on going to the restaurant where everyone knows his name, and going nowhere else, doing nothing else.

At least I tried…

WTF?

Robert has been a "willow" for awhile. [I must refrain from smart mouthing that he is more accurately labelled a willow-er.] ☹

I posted this on Rants and Raves. One person said I am really "desperate".

Craigslist Hotties (I can't wait to meet you!)

The last few days I've noticed an HIV+ man who will not date BBW and an ex-convict who also will not date BBW. Today, one was even better - he's married (of course) and is looking for a Lady GaGa type. He wants to live vicariously through her. Unfortunately for the HIV+ guy and the convicted felon I am "too fat" for them. I'm not a BBW, but I also need to lose a few extra pounds. You might even say more than "a few." Unfortunately for the Lady GaGa lover, I am too old (as well as "too fat") and would never wear clothing made from meat. Good luck on your searches for Miss Right!

Almost as soon as it went live, someone flagged and removed this:

"We could have gone to the Paw Paw Festival together!

I didn't have anyone to accompany me to the Paw Paw Festival this week-end, so I drove down by myself. Although it was enjoyable, it would have been more fun with a companion.

You:

Over 40

Loves life

Single!!!

Likes the outdoors

Me:

Over 40

Loves life

Single, kids grown and independent

Loves the outdoors, reading, animals"

The one person who beat the clock sent the following email message: "do you have a pic"   He didn't even bother with a question mark.

Keep it positive!! Another competitor in Cyber Love spent two paragraphs describing her basement pool table and as for herself, she said she was overweight, but losing, something I would never say. (We are already perfect!) We are what we are today, and let tomorrow take care of itself. It also sounds like you are trying too hard. In addition, she mentioned the property she owns and that her mother is her best friend and lives with her. Dating is similar to interviewing for a job, in that there are many candidates, and therefore people are looking for reasons to exclude possibilities. You don't want to be weeded out before the first round, do you? You also do not want a fortune hunter stealing your heart, and your bank account. So, leave out your living arrangements and your possessions. That is your business and has nothing to do with going out on a casual date. A good relationship starts out with a casual date and keeps growing.

On a whim I decided to conduct a little experiment by answering several ads placed by middle aged men claiming to be highly educated, healthy, active and athletic, connoisseurs of the finer things in life and able to afford them. In short, Renaissance men. Advertising on free dating sites. Looking for the perfect woman. Liars, anyone?

First, I set up a special email account with a fake name. Then I ran an Internet search for a picture of the perfect woman to fit the profile. No facial shot (excuse: I don't send pictures that would identify me to anonymous men) but merely the back of my head down to my knees. I am wearing two tank tops and a pair of shorts showing serious plumber crack. I am also - shock, gasp, everyone hates a fat woman - at least fifty pounds overweight, most of it settled happily in my derriere.

You would think men with so much to offer would ignore me, but they did not.

I attached the not really me picture and mailed the following introductory message from the not really me email address:

Your ad interested me. I like to think that I am feminine (but not too frou frou) and pleasant. I love cooking for my man.

I am interested in all areas of health/fitness and will be starting a body building class in a few weeks. I attended high school until I got married in my junior year. Unfortunately, the relationship didn't last, but I do have four beatuiful [sic] children that mean the world to me.

☠⚰_____

WTF?

Why is this so difficult? All he wants is to meet a woman born in May. No smokers. ☹

21

The British (Non) Invasion

They all say they'll cross the pond to meet me, and I always believe them, at first, and they never do.

Neville was honest. Don't trust an Englishman until you see the whites of his eyes. He was divorced, involved with his kids and candid about his romantic past. Chatting every evening (my time) we were buddies, chums, cohorts, comrades, and mates and he candidly admitted that long distance friendship was all he had to offer. The charm, excitement, fantasy, fascination, glamour and mystery of True Love was no longer of any consequence to him.

Unlike my pseudo suitors, he actually did walk up the steps of a big silver bird and land in the New Country to meet the girl of his dreams. He picked her out of the welcoming crowd and "I knew the minute I got off the plane I wasn't interested in her." However, he was a practical man and decided to make the most of his one week vacation. He enjoyed watching her big screen tv in a big comfy chair, ate good food and had sex with her. He was cheerful and friendly the entire visit and never spoke to her again after he returned home. And he was/is one of the good men! He and I enjoyed chatting and when he decided Internet dating wasn't worth the $25 or so a month, he told me beforehand he was shutting it down. He also told me to keep my powder dry and to hold out for Mr. Right.

Cairns, the ever popular Scottish gentleman, a legend in his own mind, sent me one photo (his wedding in 1975). Plaid - he wore a kilt on his big day - is no more flattering on a man than it is on a woman. He called me at 3:30 in the morning, his time, apparently to argue. He hates dogs and he hates cats, he hates my favorite 60s British singers. Before he would visit me, he must be sure that I will find homes for my pets. When I tried to explain that I love my pets and could never get rid of them he said I was stubborn. I have to have my own way. Then: I'm chubby He doesn't like chunky, dumpy women.

Looking at his thirty year old wedding picture, I thought he looked stout and stubby, well on his way to tubby, especially for such a young man. Personality is more important to me than looks, so his height and weight were not deal breakers on my part. If it had worked out I'd have considered him My Cuddly Bunny.

The ultimate insult and conversation closer consisted of him telling me that he has visited America before, he has girlfriends all over the United States, and they are better looking than I am, and to be honest, he would never visit me. But I still should get rid of my pets. And stop being so obstinate, unyielding and unreasonable.

No man wants a controlling woman.

    Clive, a caulkhead (descended from long-established island stock), a sweetheart of a man, lived on the Isle of Wight, located in the English Channel, known for its festivals, dinosaur fossils and wildlife (fauna, not parties). Amicably divorcing after a long marriage, he didn't have a lot of money, but he wanted to spend Christmas Eve with me, over the phone. It was a delightful conversation. Had I not have a 200 year old taproot keeping me home, or if I had a sense of adventure (life does wear some of us down), I would have traveled to England to meet him. Any woman would be lucky indeed to love a man like him. P.S. He resembled Phil Collins on a very good day.

    I was so happy with an email from my British suitor, a London cop named Terrence: "I think I'm besotted by you. No, I am besotted by you. xxxx" This wonderful man and I chatted every day, and even used a webcam. I hate getting my picture taken! The harsh light washes me out. Still, my long blonde hair enticed him. He's cute but convinced he is not. I missed several exercise sessions, due to our time difference. He promised to fly over to meet me. Oh, you're ahead of me, aren't you?

    The inevitable Dear Jane letter arrived, but he doesn't understand that is what it is. He is so happy, because since pre-pubescent days he has been in love with The Girl That Got Away, and now they are both divorced after long marriages.

She has MS, but instead of it killing her last February as he had told me would happen (why would he think I would want her to die?), her disease has gone into remission. They spent the weekend at a hotel, he bought her a diamond, and they shall wed next spring. Oh, but before I feel left out, I was assured I would receive an invite!! Glad I learned my lesson and didn't waste time on him or take anything seriously. I guess his promise of coming over here was a typical man thing. But I do regret wasting time chatting with him when I could have been outdoors.

One thing I learned about the British is this: contrary to their cold and reserved reputations, it is common for them to sign emails and letters "XOXO." This is generic and does not mean that the person is madly in love with you. A female friend sends me birthday and Christmas cards from across the pond, and it is safe to assume she is not interested in pursuing a romance with me.

The last man I was seriously interested in became disinterested in me when I admitted my interest in him (after he spent hundreds of dollars on transatlantic cell phone calls). Is this logical? Does this make any sense? Do you have the heart for all this? If I would have played by the rules, he would probably be by my side right now. However, another, craftier woman, now "owns" his heart. They met when he was married, an owner of an auto body shop, living in an expensive house. After his separation, this woman dumped him saying, "your wife drives a better car and she got the house." He lived in a cheap apartment while having a new house built, and romanced me via phone, and yes, as the house neared completion, the other woman called him, wanting him back. He chose her over me. We are all within the same age range.

Iorwerth called me frequently, drunkenly telling me he loved me to bits, before confessing that me the woman ("the waitress" that wasn't good enough for him, a business owner - what a jerk) wanted him back.

The idea of a Welshman romancing me was – romantic! Even his name sent me on a flight of fancy. Iorwerth! Picture him, moody and mysterious, calling me at all hours, drinking heavily but never drunk. Sigh.

Iorwerth reminded me Richard Burton, one of Elizabeth Taylor's husbands (twice) with his love of red wine. It's heart healthy! Drink up!

I love daffodils? I'm in luck, then, for they are the official flower of Wales. There are thousands blooming every spring in his hometown.

I learned the proper pronunciation of "Celtic." Boston basketball game or no, "Kelltic" it is, "Selltic" it is not.

When I go to Wales, don't admit to being of Irish descent or people will think me a simpleton. He explained "Irish logic." [The term is an oxymoron, as we have none.] And for Cripes' sake, never confess having a drop of German blood. No one in Great Britain has ever or will ever forget WWII. My birth name and my married name, difficult to pronounce and sometime referred to as "funny" are both dead giveaways of my heritage.

Iorwerth was on the fence about visiting me and needed a little encouragement so I drove around to pick up brochures from little pieces of Americana: 1880s working farm/metro park, covered bridges,

At an air show, I picked up a large pack of 100 Years of Airpower postcards and dutifully sent out one a day. He loved airplanes and even if he didn't, it was a good man type gift.

Internet dating is no different than real time courting. A woman giving too much lowers her value. It's not fair, but it's life.

I made a total fool of myself, sending him American racing magazines (we did share a lot of auto racing) along with the brochures of local points of interest. I bought pink printer paper, loaded up clip art into a graphics program, and made Two Tickets to Paradise to be redeemed by bearer only, in person.

You don't need to know the details about *The Passion Gazette*, also printed out on pink paper. To call it sexy would be a great overstatement. It was just a lonely, silly woman's childish attempt to – ahem – warm his "heart." He loved it, but he never boarded a plane to the United States to claim my hand.

He, being a Smart Man, looked down on me, a silly half Irish woman. How did I find out? When he accidentally sent an email to me with a picture of my car, entitled "Posh Car, No Brains." Who's the one with no brains, Iorwerth? Who was your intended recipient?

We spent a lot of time arguing about my inability-unwillingness to iron clothing. After spending my childhood watching my mother sprinkle clean clothes with water, roll them up and refrigerate for a day, then sweat and worry about having a heatstroke, I buy wrinkle free dresses, jeans, shirts and skirts. If a man needs sharp pressed pants and dress shirts, he is free to drop them off at a dry cleaning establishment. (See next paragraphs for the resolution of this hopeless romance.)

Toward the end of The Big Romance Iorwerth told me he was considering getting a mail order bride from a third world country. These women were "stunning." I am not. His brother obtained (purchased, one might say) a much younger wife in that manner, and the only hitch was that he would have to send money home to the woman's family. The brother's wife cooked, cleaned, ironed (!), took care of him sexually, and kept her mouth shut. Even though the in-laws needed financial support, they lived far, far away and were of no consequence.

Then – "the waitress" reappeared. At first he fought this Great Love, but eventually gave in.

Although I took it that way, the fact that we were both reading "M is for Malice" did not mean it was a sign from God, or Cupid, that we would be able to overcome the Atlantic Ocean, his "dynamic" personality, my refusal to iron, his love for the woman who was involved in his divorce and his desire to buy a housekeeper/cook/laundress/lover.

A friend said that Iorwerth looked like he had been ridden hard and put away wet (her kind way of suggesting he might drink a wee bit much) and that she feared he would break my heart.

He did.

And we never even met.

You'd think that would be enough punishment, but no, I kept wishin' and hopin' and loggin' on, even getting up in the middle of the night to check my email.

Onto chatting with a London cop who found me on a site devoted to the dead! He found my husband's tribute and decided to contact me. How much time did I waste on him? You don't want to know. He still emails me.

I met another guy through the same dedicated to the deadsite, but at least he lived within five or six miles of my house, and we actually met and went out on a few dates, before he said being attracted to me made him feel like a pervert. He's two months older than my daughter. It didn't bother me, and as I recall when we had a picnic and went on a hike, we had a great time. He even told me it was the best date he had had, maybe ever. We were never "romantically" involved, but he was cute and we are still in contact. He texted me a few days ago, in the middle of the night, just to see if I were ok. Of course he had an ulterior motive for calling! But it's still flattering.

WTF?

SWPM, athletic, mentally and financially sound, willing to travel to meet a lactating female for the romantic experience of a lifetime. ☹

22

One Phone Call Was One Too Many

I landed a carp and threw him back.

My last site was www.theoceansarefullofit.com. That's not the real name, but it's close enough. Shortly after baiting my hook and casting the line, I got a nibble. Correction - it was a shark attack!

"You're adorable. Wanna get married?"

Thinking he was joking, I responded, "Thanks for the chuckle."

No, seriously...

Fool that I am and wanting to hear what he said to say I gave him my phone number.

To make a long story short:

What's a paralegal? Someone who rides in an ambulance? No, I work in a law office.

Oh, that's what my third wife does. She helped me get my fourth divorce. He was serious.

Elmer tells jokes. I hate that. The amusing story about three nuns was not funny. It was vulgar. I'm not a prude but when I didn't laugh he accused me of having no sense of humor. "I don't like it when someone I don't know starts talking about sex."

He moved to Buffalo to marry a woman he met online, but that lasted only two years. All his wives are drunks and cheaters. The last one shoplifted a lipstick from Walmart in front of him.

Since his last divorce, he has met about ten women. He stayed the night with two of them - separately of course - and the next morning said, "I'm sorry but I can't love you."

Elmer is a romantic. He misses being married. He thinks I am the woman for him.

He asked what happened to my marriage to which I replied, "That is my marriage and my husband isn't here to tell his side of it and I don't discuss it with anyone."

I ended the conversation with "I have to go clean the kitchen." A tumbler of ruby red grapefruit juice with a splash of vodka, the history channel turned on, Martha Stewart Living on the nightstand, and Eddie cuddled by my side, and I'm ready to visit Mr. Sandman so I can greet another day.

One guy lost me in his first sentence. "Carol? This is Dennis, from plenty of feesh (fish)." Ok, call me superficial, call me bitchy, call me silly, call me ridiculous, but I am not listening to a man who pronounces fish as "feesh." He probably also says "poosh." A beloved relative was married to a man with a similar accent. He was an abusive drunk and perhaps this makes me think of him. I can't remember this particular man's name so I am going to refer to him as "Dennis." Dennis was the first guy I ever dated, and believe me, if I could find him (an intellectual red haired guy with a superiority complex), and he would have me, we would be back in business. And, yes, I have run several Internet searches looking for him. He hasn't popped up anywhere, including the social security death index, so I know he's out there somewhere…but not on a quest for me.

Black Flag

"I hope this site works better than the others." ☹

A phone call I received from a cyber suitor we'll call Dean went thusly: Carol?

Me: Yes

D: This is Dean from the Internet. Before this goes any further, how old is your picture?

Me: About a year.

D: There is a lot of deception over the Internet, and I always insist on a recent picture.

Me: I don't have any pictures, but we could talk over a webcam. I don't have anything to hide.

(Don't you hate "dates" reminiscent of job interviews?)

D: You're 5'3". You don't burn many calories and you don't

need to eat as much as you do. And you should hit the treadmill at least an hour a day. At least. And don't eat as much.

Me: In good weather, I walk four ---

Realizing I owe no one any explanations about any part of my life, I hung up the phone before finishing the sentence. For the record, I am overweight, although I do eat healthily and walk two to four miles a day, weather and time permitting. I am of the endomorph persuasion and a woman with a stocky build will never be fragile and frail. Ectomorph lovers need to keep on walkin'.

He did not call back, but he did email me at the dating site. I deleted Mr. Charm's message before reading it.   I also deleted my profile from this site.

This attempt at romance did not go well.

A 64 old contacted me from plentyoffish.com, and since the same 32 year old texted me that day, and has been talking to me since he was 28, a 64 year old seems ancient to me.

Bennie called me within minutes after I gave him my phone number.

Unfortunately, I was in the midst of attempting to figure out how to complete my taxes. I had tried several weeks before and couldn't figure out one line, so I put it off. At that time, my first go around, I owed more than my annual salary. On to another tax site which estimated a $37 refund.   For some reason this time I owed almost $250. As bad as the amount due was, I just wanted to get it over.

Bennie lives east of town on Route "222." Not to argue (and I didn't) but as a lifelong resident I know it is Route "22" not "222." Always looking for a common interest, I told him I kept up with the saga of Bozo a canine officer shot twice and left for dead. Although Bozo was paralyzed, through excellent veterinary care, rehabilitation and the grace of God, he recovered. I probably do talk about Bozo too much, but he inspires me!

Bennie interrupted me. He is an old hippie, and he doesn't particularly like cops. Who doesn't like a story about a dog surviving against all odds? Then he started in about San Francisco in the 60s, which is of zero interest to me. It's 2012!!

While I was working on my taxes and simultaneously listening to him ("uh, uh...yes...uh, uh..."), I heard a knock-down drag-out cat fight in the back bedroom. Before I had the chance to run toward the catters, my phone dropped the call.

I ran back, with my beloved Eddie and John John barking like lunatics, screaming at the cats (Remero cannot get along with any other males) and throwing a plastic plate to separate them. On the way back to my taxes, I stopped in the kitchen long enough to see that my spaghetti dinner was scorched.

The theme from SVU went off, then the message alert, then the phone again, then another message alert. One short message: "What happened?" followed by one consisting of background noise, his tv blaring. He didn't say a word.

With all this, speaking to an old hippie was last on my list. I put on my Kasey Kahne jammies, then hit the hay with a magazine filled with pictures of English gardens.

Oh, and I forgot to add that he is going to date a string of women before he finds the right one that he will stay with forever.

One local lad posted his picture circa 1966. How can I pinpoint the exact year? Because his glasses, suit and hairstyle looked just like my dead husband's high school graduation picture! When he asked me what kind of problems I had, I told him my house needed a lot of work. The house was in bad shape? Yes. Not my family? No family problems? Just things that could be fixed? Just things that can be repaired. His problem was much more serious, and I needed to know about it. He had joint custody of his 14 year old daughter. He just found out she was dating someone he didn't approve of. He believed she was having sex with the guy, who was 19. The boyfriend was of a different race. He hated to have to do it, but he was desperate: he beat his daughter. However, she was totally out of control and continued to be with the man. Then he asked me if I would like to go out with him. I didn't even bother to make up an excuse to keep from hurting his feelings, instead suggesting he might need to concentrate on his family.

Elmer was a businessman who wanted to wine and dine me. However, his honesty – and we all demand honesty, don't we? – scared me off. He is financially stable (and the more men I am exposed to, the more I realize how rare this is among single men), lived within twenty miles of my house, divorced, friendly, and emotionally available (ditto on being a rare quality). However, before he asked me out, there was something I needed to know about him, something that puts most women off: he transports stiffs for a living. This is my terminology as I don't know what the official term for his chosen occupation would be. When he told me he is an independent contractor who charges $300 a body to remove the deceased from nursing homes to the friendly neighborhood mortuary, it extinguished any possible flames. He is on call 24/7. Since he lives in a metropolitan area, and there aren't workers knocking down doors to ply this trade, his business has a successful bottom line. When I told a friend about this, she said I should not exclude him only because of his profession, and that he probably has interesting stories to tell. (???????) While I was not overly encouraging, I gave him the option of calling me again to make a date for pizza. He never phoned again. For the right person, he is a good catch, but the thought of anyone who works with dead bodies in any capacity touching my very alive body makes my skin crawl. Would it bother you?

One man that is still advertising and I traded a few emails. If his pictures are to be believed he is attractive, but we never met due to severe weather conditions (apparently he couldn't wait a few days for snow covered, icy roads to clear). He states he is attractive, professional, a home owner, possesses a car and a driver's license (good for him! No, scrub, he!). Going through a divorce, he wants a woman to move in with him and contribute to the household income (otherwise he will lose his house). You must be physically attractive and intelligent. I do believe you will be blessed with helping raise his teen-ager daughter if you are The Chosen. I wonder if "we" will pay her college tuition, too.

    Perhaps the worst rejection came from Richie, from Alaska. He wasn't movie star handsome, but he looked reliable. He called me several times (complaining about the phone bill) and we talked for at least an hour. "Are you working magic spells? I can't stop thinking about you..." He offered to ride his trusty cycle down through Canada on his vacation, bedroll on the back. I was better looking than his previous girlfriend. Then -- you wouldn't like it here. He felt the need to explain Seasonal Affective Disorder to me, which wasn't necessary as I suffer it every year in Ohio. Think of how much worse it would be in Alaska! But Alaska is gorgeous country! His kids might not want me living with him. Finally: Your breasts are too big. Dumb women have big breasts. I am an intelligent men and it would embarrass me to be with you. I knew I would never move to Alaska, so perhaps I wasn't as stupid as he would like to think.

23

Checking Out the Ads

One guy who advertises quite frequently is the right age, single, educated, attractive (enough) - and too picky! He is a faithful Christian of a denomination that he considers the only valid church. He is also a political conservative who is looking for a woman that might not exist (as are some of us women are searching for the elusive Mr. Right). When I responded to his ad telling him that I am a non-denominational Christian, at home at any church, Protestant or Catholic, and don't even need to attend services, he told me that this was not what he wants. The woman of his dreams must see God in exactly the same light as he does (the only way, according to him). The fact that I am not a conservative (although several friends have told me that I hold conservative "values" and I would never argue politics with anyone) also puts me in the reject pile. I will not be hearing from him again.

His latest ad gave me a laugh. Ms. Right still must be a conservative, fundamentalist Christian of his denomination, not something similar, but now he wants any interested females to realize they are not getting sex before marriage and he will not drive them around. Don't even ask! It makes one wonder what kind of responses he received to make him add those two stipulations. Did a Bad Girl try to trade sexual favors for rides in his car? How shocked was he? Just how wild and wicked was this woman? Was his car a four door American made sedan? It would be fun to imagine him driving around in a foreign sports car. Did he have to fight for his honor? Did she try to seduce him? Did she light up a cigarette? Did she suggest they go to a bar? Did she want to go dancing? Did she use Bad Words? Did she have dyed hair? Wear too much make-up? Dress like a Jezzebell? Since belonging to his church is a deal-breaker, why doesn't he look around his congregation? He's there three times a week. Or why doesn't he volunteer in the next election? I couldn't imagine where he might find a woman that would absolutely refuse to have sex before marriage, but would want to fulfill her wifely duties after their Day of Days, but there might be one or two who demand taxi service.

The heading of one man's heading – you know, how you entice people – read, "Want to go hoggin'."

Hogging. Are you aware of this term? I had never heard that expression before in my entire 38 years (a little levity on my part) traversing this earth, but here's what he has to say:

Every guy should go hoggin' at least once, and he wants to see what the big (big! get it?) fuss is about.

He is looking for a fat girl, for a no strings attached, one time only bang-a-rama. He wants a fat girl, but not nasty; neat, and not sloppy. She must be drug and disease free.

He is willing to host, which means she will travel to his place, or more likely, he will pay for a motel. Since it is a no strings attached one time only experience, there is no mention of dinner or a movie.

He does not include a picture of his own as he is a professional but all interested women must send him pictures, preferably in lingerie, which he will review. If he doesn't respond, it's because he's found the one lucky girl or the woman is not attractive enough for his hoggin' adventure.

He stresses that he is all man, and this offer is real.

When I showed a friend this ad, she said that surely no one would respond. *Au contraire*, I believe there are women that will, and perhaps even let this unromantic jerk go hoggin' all over their bodies.

At first glance, hoggin' is perhaps the rudest, cruelest "dating" I've ever heard of. However, at least the potential hog master was upfront about his motives.

Anger Management, Anyone? This man states that every woman over 40 is disgusting, fat and ugly. He wants to know if we are hoping for a blind man, or if we just want to give the man a heart attack. Perhaps we should back our sorry butts away from the all you can eat buffets. We've let ourselves go, yet we insist on a man who is fit and athletic. Do we plan on sitting him, crushing his legs, soul and all hope? He concludes by telling us to devour another Big Mac with fries and leave him alone. I just poured out a diet grape soda, and will be thrilled to ignore his (pathetic) existence.

☠🖱_____

WTF?

Dwarf tossing anyone? He wants a tinny [I guess "tiny" is too difficult for him to spell] girl. You'll earn bonus points if you like to be picked up, carried, and flung around. ☹

A man in his fifties, 6'2", 200 pounds, college educated. Sounds good, doesn't he? Oh, but due to unspecified misfortunes and mishaps (nothing illegal or immoral, he hastens to reassure us), he has a modest income. Nothing wrong with that. The economy has had not been kind of many of us, including yours truly. However, here's the rub: he is looking for a wealthy lady to fund their life together, traveling. She should own a boat or be willing to purchase one (but she should feel free to keep the title in her name as he is not a fortune hunter) This man is not asking for a rowboat, either. It would have a galley, sleeping quarters, and a bath with shower. Ms. Right would also need to have the time and money for extended trips. Many people assume he is lawyer, college professor, or psychiatrist due to his wardrobe purchased from an exclusive haberdashery, deportment, and command of the English language.

Having worked for attorneys, I am thinking – why would anyone looking for romance try to impersonate a lawyer, most of whom are not charming, enchanting, alluring or dreamy?

He must not have found a sucker – excuse me, I meant to say "the girl of his dreams" - because he continued his search with another ad. This time he wants an attractive woman of German or British descent, at least 5'7", no larger than size 8. And wealthy. He will direct her life for her and be a loyal companion. He requires a woman who drives a Lexus. [There are advantages to being a woman of humble means, too short and size 10.] She will share her abundance with him, including cruises and a boat. What's with the mandatory boat and cruise? Is he planning to murder her, then toss her body overboard and live off her money until he finds the next victim?

A "nice looking businessman" wants to take attractive women shopping at Victoria's Secret. He pays, and you choose the mall. The catch: he gets to watch you model the lingerie in the store. We can only assume he's married, and this is his way of fulfilling his fantasies without "cheating." If you are young and gorgeous and careful you might be able to have fun.

MW professional M looking for companionship. His wife is the most boring person in the entire world. He would like to meet someone with a sense of adventure. No promises.

One guy is open to a LTR with the right woman, or more specifically, the right pair of feet. He's not into pain or chains (????) but he wants to remove your shoes and kiss your feet, then give you a loving foot massage at the end of the work day. Age and race are not important to him. I had corresponded with a man with a foot fetish previously, and I still have no interest. My feet are ugly! I walk! It's difficult enough keeping hands soft and smooth (and for several winter months each year, it is nearly impossible), and I am not going to worry about my feet being attractive enough for a romantic encounter.

One man's ad stated he was Christian, in his 50s, divorced and looking for a wife. He doesn't smoke, drink, curse or chase other women. In addition to attending church regularly, he enjoys the outdoors, camping, fishing, picnics, romantic walks. He loves kids and dogs. He appreciates women for all the work they do, especially everything in the home. He isn't a picky eater, likes most music, drives a practical car, and is a disabled veteran. Love is God's gift to us. Sounds really nice, almost to the point of being boring, right? Wrong! He finally admits to be "oversexed" (whatever that means). He wants his wife to tease him by wearing nothing underneath her dress. He's not boring, he's fun! A normal looking woman is good enough for him. No giant bosom (expletives deleted) required! However, this is the deal breaker: You must not groom your nether regions or he would have to break up with you, no matter how serious his intentions were. He then describes his male anatomy in great detail. No, I didn't read all of it. I couldn't. Are you the one to make his heart pound with anticipation? I know I'm not. P.S. I cleaned up his language, quite radically.

☠🖱_____

WTF?

I am very sorry for not getting back to you right away. My computer screen was dirty and I thought you had a missing front tooth. Anyway, after I wiped my monitor I looked at your pic again. You are gorgeous!!! Please contact me again - I would love to take you to Jamaica! ☹

His ad states he is already dating four "nice" ladies and is looking for a fifth. He wants a different woman, Monday through Friday nights, and then two lucky ladies will be chosen from the five to spend Saturday and Sunday with him. He hastens to add that one is for Saturday, the other for Sunday, not two at a time. He would not anyone to think he is a jerk. He has a job and is fun-loving. At least he isn't married. Do you think the ladies know about each other? What is the criteria for being chosen as one of the week-end women? Is Saturday or Sunday the plum date? Where does he get his stamina? Not just sexually, but where does he get the energy to go out every night of the week? When does he have time to do his laundry? Does he pay for dinner or do the women go dutch treat?

One man states he is looking for a second wife. This one I could not figure out - is he a bigamist or serial husband? He said you should be open minded, and he will give you all the love and sex and romance you could ever want, and that you deserve his kind attentions. He does require that you have a job. I wonder if his first wife will also shower you with love, sex, romance and attention. Do you each provide a home, and he takes turns visiting you the way Grandma gets passed around? Or does he have a place of his own? *Menage a trois*? No, thanks.

Bigamy Buford is honest, kind, fun, educated, easy going, doesn't smoke or drink. His kids are grown, and he and his first wife want to have a second wife to join their fabulous life. He doesn't care how old you are as long as you have a good heart. If you think you could fit in, please contact him. Well, Johnny Baby, as it happens I don't think I want to fit in, and neither would most other women, so don't spend too much time checking your email.

WTF?

Self-described cute guy with a beer gut wants a girl with a big juicy ass who thinks for herself, the crazier the better. Don't mention your obsession with Brangelina, the Kardashians or The Royal Family or he will not respond. ☹

Hector doesn't expect Barbie but don't take that to mean that Rosie O will win his affections. She must replace her pets and grown children with the only important thing in her life – HIM. He is drama-free, fit and healthy, and you must not be a bitter, suspicious witch. Perhaps he's left a woman or two a bit disillusioned? He doesn't want a pen pal (that's a plus) so Ms. HWP should be ready to meet him. Mr. Congeniality wants you to know that he will be treating you to neither a free meal NOR sex on a first date. He might be shocked to find out that very few women want anything from him.

WTF?

No car, no truck, not even a bicycle, no income, but he is neat and clean, d/d free. He can't afford to smoke, and drinks when he has money. He will not pay for a third party website to view your naked arse. No BBWs. Sorry. Good luck! ☹

A starseed who looks at least ten years younger than his chronological age of 50 is looking for you – if you are also from another planet. Yes, you read that right. He's a 21st century extraterrestrial. (No word on what planet or galaxy he came from or why he decided to come to Planet Earth.) A true renaissance man, he's caring, supportive, athletic, adventurous, clever, creative, enterprising, ingenious, intelligent, inventive, original, quick-witted, sharp, talented,, intelligent, insightful, educated, philharmonic, and soft spoken. He loves all animals, especially cats. He finds long walks delightful. If you aren't a fellow space traveler on a mission to help raise spiritual awareness, you are not The One. I emailed him, thinking perhaps we could discuss our unique perspectives of life, but he was not interested. I think I was too old. Or too fat.

Weighty Matters. To some, "a few extra pounds" is criminal. This is an actual quote from an ad: "No BBW's, one night stands, invitations to pay sites or prostitutes." Please notice that BBW is first on the Public Enemy List, well before prostitute. Many other men either don't have a type or like a little meat on the bones, considering curves feminine. Imagine that!

The last few days I've noticed an HIV+ man who will not date BBW and an ex-convict who also will not date BBW. Today, one was even better - he's married (of course) and is looking for a Lady GaGa type. He wants to live vicariously through her. Unfortunately for the HIV+ guy and the convicted felon I am "too fat" for them. I'm not a BBW, but I also need to lose a few extra pounds. You might even say more than "a few." Unfortunately for the Lady GaGa lover, I am too old (as well as "too fat") and would never wear clothing made from meat. Good luck on your searches for Miss Right!

A Stephen King look-alike wants a petite, intelligent and opened minded to being with a young lady to my body type. Please be cute and intelligent and open-minded to my androgynous personality. He's a cuddlebug.

WTF?

From a woman who knows this dangerous freak: He posts that children are welcome but he is really looking for little girls to pose in pantyhose for him. The mother of a ten year old reported him to the police. I've read several ads that scream pedophile! If you have children, please be extra cautious. ☹

Spell Check, Anyone? This is a nice guy looking for a relationship, not a one-night stand. However, you will have to interpret what he means by describing himself as a "profical clown."

Oh! Professional! I get it. So, I'm a little slow on the uptake. Clowns scare some of us.

Fifty-five year old SWM, wants a professional female (MBA preferred) who loves pushing her employees around, then going home to be spanked and dominated any way he pleases during rough sex.

His polar opposite is in desperate need of a mistress to serve. He doesn't know what the limits are in a such a relationship and hopes Mistress Right can help him expand his horizons. He's normal height and weight and has blond hair.

A man who loves kissing and cuddling and oral sex (he doesn't specify if this goes both ways) is looking for a retirement age woman who has not been involved "romantically" for years. She must host, daytime only. NSA.

I didn't qualify for a chance with this man as I am too "old": He will consider only women between 30 and 52 who send pictures. He emphasizes that pictures are mandatory. In return he is 5'11", handsome, loving, caring, truthful, and faithful. He will pamper the right woman. He likes watching movies as well as sitting and talking. "Handsome" is a subjective term, so we'll leave that determination to others, but according to the picture on his profile the man is morbidly obese. I'm no one to judge weight because I could stand to lose a good twenty pounds, but my activities are more physical than sitting and talking. As with anyone, we wish the man well in his quest.

According to his profile, Boyd doesn't watch much television, but he feels compatibility could be predicted by favorite shows. It makes sense (in a way) but wouldn't seem to be a deal breaker. He then lists reality shows in order of preference. If your tastes don't match, move on to someone else. He claims to look at least twenty years younger than his actual age and has been compared favorably with Burt Reynolds. ????!!!!!! What year is this? 1977 or 2012? To land this fabulous catch, you must be romantic, have long hair, weigh less than 200 pounds and have a good set of headlights. No strings attached, but he will buy you dinner and will drive you around in his nice car.

Alan, a white, divorced, self-employed professional male, is seeking his very own domestic goddess. He requires a playful, honest, intelligent, monogamous, sexy woman who enjoys taking care of him and his home instead of working for a living. He's fun, loving and successful. No mention of a ring on her finger.

Here's a real sweetheart: He wants an attractive woman that is not overweight. His upper limit is 120 pounds. If you are insulted, log off and hit the gym. He ends his ad by reiterating and emphasizing that he does not want a hippopotamus. Keeping in the animal genre, I will add that most of us do not want a jackass.

Santa is hoping to find a fun-loving, sexy elf to keep him company in the Caribbean for a week of sunshine. Santa is 60, but although he doesn't list age, height or weight restrictions, a picture will get the (snow)ball rolling. However, I would never go on a trip with a stranger and the words "too good to be true" flashed through my mind, or what is left of it.

♥ ▶▶ _____

Reminder: If someone doesn't have drama in his life, he isn't hoping that some woman will come along and start arguments, cause trouble and generate an emotional whirlwind, tearing apart his peaceful world. A calm man appreciates a (reasonably) serene woman. Don't confuse "exciting" with "frenetic" and "disturbed." ♥

This good ol' boy is looking for a down to earth woman, someone to go fishing, hunting, camping and hiking with him. He's slender and wants you to be, too. He does not want a woman with her hair chopped off, or "raped" up in herself and fancy clubs. He's not rude and looks fifteen years younger than his actual age.

Most of us can relate to this 44 year old man: After posting too many ads, he is giving up. Some women wouldn't recognize a good guy if he bit her on the ass. It's our loss because he loves to cuddle, he's fun loving and easy going and hard working.

Lawrence had his picture taken with his dog (I love dogs!). Other than that, he was not for me. He's not picky about looks or age, but finances are going to be split 50-50, no exceptions. He supported one wife and he's not going to do it again.

George sounds like Lawrence on steroids. What a true romantic! This divorced man is looking for a honest, caring and loving woman (no drunks or cheaters need apply) to live in. His house, which includes three large bedrooms, two and a half baths, laundry room, finished basement with a pool table, up to date kitchen, and two car garage is clean and located in a nice neighborhood close to shopping and the bus line. The lucky lady must pass a criminal background check. (I can do that.) She needs to be very sexually animated. (I'm not.) His Juliette must have a job as she will be financially responsible for half their living expenses. George is attractive and expects his mate to be HWP, preferably thin. No mention as to cleaning responsibilities but I am guessing most of it falls on the successful applicant.

☠🖱_____

WTF?

Free dinner. Oh, not for you, but for him. He has a coupon good for one free dinner with the purchase of one adult dinner. You might have to sit together, but at least you will have a dining companion and he will get a free meal. You can meet him at the door. ☹

A 70ish white stallion wants to meet a white mare that hasn't been around the track too many times. You pick the stall and he'll pay for the oats. He promises he will never run a pretty little filly too hard and then put her away wet. He is a derby contender and hopes you aren't too broad in the withers. Gallop over to the computer and shoot him an email

❤ ⏭ _____

Amore!

Baby blues, cuddling fool looking for his soul mate. He'll cook the steak if you bring the potatoes. ♥

24

Good Ones I Never Got to Meet in Person
(But I'll Love Them Forever!)

Slightly younger Kurt lived about two hours away. Divorced, a landscaper, hard working single dad with full custody of his ten year old son, whom he home schooled as the boy was a victim of bullying. The distance was difficult and we both had too many other commitments for us to ever be a couple. When I asked him if there were any girls he was attracted to in Real Life, ever a gentleman, he very reluctantly admitted there was.

Does she have blonde curly hair to her shoulders? Does she wear hair gel? Does she wear jeans to work? As he could have been a great catch I hated to push another woman onto him, but nevertheless I asked: Is she about a size five, with a cute butt?

Yes. How did I know? Don't ask me, but I could only "see" her from the back and don't know anything else about her. However, Kurt - go after her. She's adorable and perky and you would be the best thing that ever happened to her.

I never heard how this relationship worked out, but he left me with very positive feelings. Even though he had very little money, he wanted to buy me an electric blanket because he knew my house was drafty and he wanted me to stay warm that winter.

Randy lived about two hours away and since neither of us was willing to relocate, we had a short but memorable phone courtship. He spent a lot of time at the drags in the summer, something that would have interested me in my younger days, and I still like cars and racing, so we had that in common. Do you want to hear what he said to me? He gave me such a compliment that I will love him until the end of time. He said with my yellow hair and my fun clothing and make up, I would always be his little Cyndi Lauper! Damn those 120 miles! I could be at the Night of Thunder right now wearing my black handkerchief miniskirt (not too short) and my James Dean t-shirt and a pair of dollar store flip-flops having fun, just like all girls wanna. Unlike my heroine, however, I wasn't willing to drive all night to see him.

❤ ▶▶_____

Amore!

Rhett in search of his Scarlett. He does give a damn! ❤

"Where y'at?" Late one autumn afternoon while "cleaning the kitchen" (as only a childish adult can) I was pleasantly surprised to receive a phone call from New Orleans. The Big Easy, Vieux Carré (French Quarter), beignets, pralines, *A Streetcar Named Desire*... In a Louisianian accent Baptiste explained that while going through old papers he found my number. He was a little lonely. Did I have time to talk? To be honest, I didn't remember anything about him but enjoyed our conversation, our phone date, learning about his life as a chef.

Baptiste offered me recipes for Dirty Rice and Jambalayam, and explained a dish called Hobo Dinner based on the Cajun Trinity (onions, bell pepper and celery). I was tempted to catch the next flight out so I could sample his Cajun fried buttermilk mashed potato cakes, sprinkled liberally with ground cayenne pepper (the latter being my own contribution to the feast).

❤ ▸▸_____

Helpful Hint to Lovely, Loving Ladies from "Just a Guy"

Give up on your dream of a prince galloping on a white horse to whisk you away to Live Happily Ever After. It ain't gonna happen, but even if it did who's going to clean up the horse manure? Welcome to the real world and don't hurt yourself when you get off your high horse. ❤

One nice looking hard working man and I shared a birthday. Like yet another Saggittarian, Robert could be nicknamed Ol' Blue Eyes as his were his most noticeable feature. Recently divorced (drama free – it was her idea) and head of a county road crew in Iowa, the Land between Two Rivers, he was not interested in moving a few states east, so this courtship, too, was brief. However, when he learned of bad luck with rascally raccoons ravaging my garden that summer, he packed up his best beefsteak tomatoes along with a few yellows and air expressed them to me. Robert, you are one of the good guys. I hope he found a woman deserving of such a thoughtful man.

Joe was nine years younger and going through an ambush divorce. His wife had wanted the house remodeled, and since he installed doors and windows for a living, rebuild, renovate, repaired and restore he did. When he was finishing the trim in the living room he was slapped with divorce papers. Seventeen years they had been married and in all that time he had worked hard and stayed faithful.

Hearing about my home repair needs, he offered to take a working vacation and sleep on my couch. I was of course too embarrassed to allow him to do such a thing.

We chatted and emailed every day, and I'll always remember our one phone call and his authentic New Joisey accent. He said I am a real lady (which I am not), giving the example that of all the women he chatted with I am the only one that didn't play true confessions about my sex life. Complete strangers told him exactly what they did in a physical relationship, and how they liked it.

He was stocky and as many men with that build appear to be, he was fatally attracted to a woman who was thin. She had been divorced several times, might have had a drug problem, wasn't overly interested in her own children, and had financial difficulties – in other words, 180 degrees from how he chose to life his own life. An involved father, her indifferent approach to motherhood bothered him, but "she weighs 90 pounds!"

At least he was honest. Who among us hasn't been taken in by someone they think is hot. I told him I wished the best because he was one of the best, and to please be careful.

WTF?

Under platonic, this simple phrase (along with a picture neck to knees, nude): horny, drunk, now! ☹

The Date

Please look your best. You want to be the one with the option for a second date. Universally flattering colors are watermelon, aqua, and teal. Lightly applied make-up, including pink lipstick, show your prettiest face.

A dress or skirt and blouse along with high heels reinforce your femininity. It goes without saying that you are freshly showered and shampooed, your hands neatly manicured. Beauty supply stores have buffing blocks and white pencils for under your nails. Hand cream completes the easiest manicure ever.

Don't dress too sexy on a first date, unless that's exactly what you want – a hit and run with no chance of a second date. Slightly more conservative saves the day. You might want to save the artillery until later.

Spritz on a light floral or fruit scent, and wear jewelry sparingly. Some men find sparkle and bling aging.

Feminine is your goal. Sexy is not (unless you want a hit and run evening). Slightly more conservative saves the day. You might want to save the artillery until later.

If you posted a recent picture and you meet your date looking your best, odds are very favorable that he will like you. Whether or not you like him is another story.

Make-up should be subtle and spotlight your beauty. A little flirty colored eye shadow is always good.

Conversation:

1. Be pleasant

2. Smile

3. Keep things light. We don't need to argue politics this early on.

4. A first - or fiftieth - date is not the time to discuss your ex from hell's bad habits. If your date asks, say something like "he was a decent guy but we grew apart." If he is not a decent guy, you could mention he is no longer in your life.

5. Most men don't appreciate gossip about your friends or co-workers.

6. If you do talk about your job, keep it to the positive aspects and leave out the horror stories. This is sometimes difficult to accomplish.

7. If you aren't attracted to him or know you could never be, stay courteous and non-committal. If he calls you after your date you can always use the old school "my boyfriend's back" exit. This

is a polite, diplomatic and kind way of turning someone down. "I am moving to a castle in France with its own forest and I can't get good cell phone reception" is not.

8. Don't talk in detail about your family. When Mr. Wrong brought pictures of Mom and told me how wonderful she is, the already miserable date didn't get any better.

9. Of course, you don't bring a first date home, no matter how strong your feelings for him or how long you've been alone. Sex on a first date almost guarantees there will be no second.

10. If your date makes you uneasy, is rude, or isn't what he said he was, find an excuse and leave. You have your own way home - either carfare or car - so hit the road. If you are truly afraid, go to a hostess or cashier and ask if the manager (or anyone else) would walk you to your car. Don't worry about hurting his feelings. Don't worry what the restaurant staff thinks. And yes, a public place is the only place to meet for a first date. It doesn't have to be an expensive restaurant.

For an enjoyable and entertaining evening, consider a progressive dinner: drinks at the first restaurant, appetizers at the second, the main course at the third location, and a decadent dessert as your grand finale. Nothing has to be expensive. It could be as simple as a soft drink at a fast food joint, then nachos before stopping for pizza. Your dessert could be a doughnut or sundae at another fast food place. Or mix it up with fancy bistros and diners.

Historic Diner, Hogs (as in piggies) and Old Cemeteries -

the baseline for my ideal date. Every other social engagement will be compared with this one.

After sleeping in one spring Sunday morning, I transplanted daffodils from my childhood homestead to my own yard. A much needed scrubbing in the shower followed. Even though casually dressed in black cotton pants and a James Dean t-shirt, I eagerly checked my email. We were still on! He would call me when he was close to my house.

We drove through a covered bridge (Padiddle! But we did not kiss) on our way to an historic diner on a county road miles from the nearest village. Although we'd each driven past many times, we'd never stopped. Were we in for a surprise. The joint was jumpin'! We sat down at the only available table and perused the menu decorated with pictures of days of yore, and stating the diner was established in the mid 1800s.

He ordered a Reuben and fries, I, a cheeseburger with everything and fries. We wanted tasty, not healthy.

An "older" couple sat beside us. I whispered for him to take note.

We discussed pets, hiking, and life. We both love cats, but he hates dogs. He admires my way with – he means no offense – my little monsters.

After we left, I told him that I had something to tell him about the couple and that there was one correct answer. He didn't realize he would be tested.

"I went to school with that man, and most likely his wife.

He hasn't changed since the mid 60s."

Yes, he did pass the test: "You look so much younger! And you act even younger!"

We drove to a working historical 1880s farm, walking through the house where volunteers were cutting blue and white print material so they could sew their own dresses. These dresses would not flatter my figure. Matronly is not the look I'm going for.

On to the barnyard where we talked to the turkeys, explaining that they needed to make a jail break before the leaves turn colors. We couldn't tell if they understood.

The sows were nursing their piglets. We both wanted to take one home. We also told the piggies that they might want to wander away before slaughter season.

After petting the workhorses, we got back into his 140 horse four cylinder five speed red horseless carriage with the sunroof open on to our last stop of the day, my family's ancestral cemetery. I showed him the tombstone of my Revolutionary War veteran (I don't know how many greats) grandfather. We then strolled the grounds to read a few of the older stones inscribed in German, the language of the day.

I saved the best for last, though. I showed him the small grave of a girl with my birth name. She died at the age of three, and although she would be either an aunt or cousin, far, far back, I'm convinced I am little Caroline, reincarnated. No one will ever persuade me to believe otherwise. He noticed the daffodils, which I proudly confessed to planting - in this life, of course. Although they come up each year, they never bloom. How unusual is that? Did he know why the entire grave was covered with stone, including the coffin shape on top of a foundation? No, and he'd never seen anything like it before. Neither had I. "Maybe they wanted to make sure I stayed put."

On the way back to the car – alas, our date was coming to an end – I pointed out a "buzzard" atop an old stone. He didn't make fun of me, but very patiently explained that it was not an eagle, buzzard or bird of any kind, but instead an urn with a covering. What I saw as a wild turkey wattle was actually a handle of the urn.

He drove me home, and there was absolutely no pressure on me to "pay" for our date. We were also confident we would speak often and regularly and spend other pleasant afternoons together.

It's too bad that the best date of my life was with a gay guy younger than my own son! But the man of my dreams is going to have to be able to provide a similarly interesting afternoon.

That afternoon inspired me to place a new ad. Win a date with me at country diner! Four men responded: a 28 year old All-American boy who would never be interested in spending time with me for any reason, a 49 year old divorced guy who lived close by (but set his controls to filter out anyone older than himself when I went to the website to view his profile), a 28 year old Asian, and a retired man who emailed me stating he was the winner, and would meet me at noon on Friday at said diner. Romantic, but not possible. He said I could pick another time. I'm going! He won! The 49 year old could have won, but if I am out of his age range, I'm out of his age range. The 28 year old Asian also won. It's just a meal.

On your date, wear lightly scented, feminine cologne and apply make-up with a gentle touch. It's very tempting to go all out but it will come off more "whole hog" or desperation than flattering, to either him or you.

A good fitting, push up bra makes your girls shine. This isn't false advertising because most of the men (we hope!) will never have the privilege of viewing your secret garden. But a sexy bra gives you confidence and draws attention to one of your best features and is well worth the money. Watch for specials, so that you can indulge yourself every day. At the very least, a good bra will erase years from your figure, and most possibly will make you more feminine and alluring.

Think "bouncy!" Bouncy breasts, bouncy hair = lively = fun = sexy! If you are under 35 or over 75, you can pull this off.

If you have a "normal" dating background, including bad relationships and sad break-ups, you have enough scepticism to keep you from being lead down the garden path. On the other hand, if you had what you describe as the perfect marriage, and your late husband is a saint, you might need to be extra careful about getting involved again. While you could be lucky the second time around, many widowed men and women have been burned. Whether they were in a rebound situation, believing the new mate would step into the deceased's shoes, or being involved with definitely the wrong person, the marriage was an eye-opener. Please consider taking your time to mourn the death of your past. After you have healed, your outlook on life could have changed, and you will be looking for different.

One man was bitterly disappointed in me, as he was expecting me to replace the love of his life, a Suzanne Sommers lookalike.

If you were left with a settlement or insurance money, keep this info to yourself. To men who ask how much life insurance a husband had, the answer is "he worked very hard for every dollar he made and he did the best he could." I personally also make it clear that I intend to continue working, regardless of any change in my marital status.

Aqua is considered a universally flattering color. It's also fresh and cheerful, so you might want to wear it on a first date. Red is exciting and alluring, so you decide if you dare!

Leave your troubles at home. A date is supposed to be fun!

The guy who is sharing the evening, or noon, or coffee break with you may be a compassionate, kind man - and we hope he is - but the first date isn't time for sob stories.

Although life would be more fair if sad, lonely people were rescued, happy women are more attractive. Yes, we've all seen women whose forced cheerfulness and laughter makes us want to scream, but did you ever notice that men seem oblivious to anything but their charisma?

This has taken a lot of experimenting, but I've finally figured out how easy it is to dress for a date. Look around at how women dress for similar outings and take it up a notch. This could mean jeans and a soft sweater. This does not mean your fussiest dress, a severe business suit to show how successful you are, or looking like you are attending a baptism. Taking it up a notch also does not mean a blouse cut down to there, or a skirt up to here, or anything too clingy, too tight, too revealing.

For a flattering, young, light-hearted and cute look, wear a denim skirt an inch or two or three above your knee. During warm weather, wear it bare legged and with sandals and a t-shirt; when it's cooler, tights, boots and a sweater.

My own personal worries at times have included financial woes (sometimes I think they are simply there, like death and taxes, and there's no sense of fussing about them), concern about the weather, fear of driving after dark, if I look good enough, why would anyone want me, I'm too "different…"

Recently at the last minute I worried about the appearance of my hands. Do they make me look old? Are they chapped? My fingernails are my weakest feature, except for my flabby tummy, but it's under wraps, at least on a first date. Polish is gorgeous and nothing is prettier than a French manicure, but with a lifestyle that includes pet care, constant (attempts at) cleaning, and gardening, any manicure doesn't last a day. So, I scrub my nails, then cream, cream, cream. But I still worry what a man will think of my hands.

Even if your tires are bald, and your engine overdue for an oil change, you're worried about your mother, and you haven't heard from your son in over a week, your checkbook is empty and payday isn't for another four days, you feel fat, and you are afraid of being rejected, smile, and enjoy yourself!

Your first date in years:

Let's get down to basics. Please don't be offended but let's not leave anything to chance.

Do wear your most attractive outfit. Aqua is considered one of the most universally flattering color, as is a shade called watermelon.

Don't dress too sexy on a first date, unless that's exactly what you want. Slightly more conservative saves the day. You might want to save the artillerary until later.

Yes, yes, yes! Make sure you, your hair, nails and clothing are sparkling clean and fresh.

Make-up should be subtle and spotlight your beauty. A little flirty colored eye shadow is always good.

One mistake, according to reliable sources (guess which gender!), some women make is wearing too much jewelry. Some men feel it is aging, others, distracting.

Flirting Tips

Keep it casual. "Hey, how's it going?" [I picked this one up from a Springsteen video]

"Did you hear about - a news item, a concert, anything of interest?"

When I was a teen-ager Scarlett O'Hara was my role model. Thinking of her surrounded by beaus at the barbecue, I used her technique of flirting with anyone within range. I practiced on random guys (no old ones, though) and found that most people enjoy the attention. You don't have to be a beauty queen, or have perfect hair and nails. You just have to be willing to brighten someone else's day. Flirting might seem manipulative or gamesmanship, but it will build your confidence so that you can relax when you are on a date with Mr. Right.

If you don't get flirting perfected, and you are a little nervous on a date, remember that this can also be attractive.

Lowering the volume and tone of your normal speaking voice, just a little, will make your conversation intimate, for his ears only. He might come a little closer to capture every syllable that flows from your kissable lips, you sexy, irresistible angel.

Keeping in mind that you are a voluptuous, inviting, spicy woman, give him a come-hither look, then smile.

Look your best. Expensive clothes, a ton of jewelry and elaborate make-up can make you appear to be trying too hard, so wear casual clothing in flattering colors to captivate and enchant.

Compliment your date. If he's a computer nerd, admire his smile, his brilliant baby blues or his pecs. He's heard about how smart he is. Conversely, if he is a pretty boy, comment on something he's said or done that confirms his intelligence. If you can't think of anything else, go for the obvious. Pretty boys do have dazzling smiles and it won't hurt for him to hear it again; IT guys are techno whizzes.

After meeting him and realizing you don't find him attractive, hide your disappointment. Be polite – unless he is rude or abusive – and smile. Hold up your end of a friendly conversation.

If he is cute, gaze into his eyes for a few seconds, smile, then look away. Play with your hair, if you dare.

Body language experts suggest your mirror the other person's movements, but it seems too contrived and I could never pull it off. Perhaps you can.

Cheat Sheet:
- Be pleasant.
- Smile.
- Keep things light. We don't need to argue politics this early on.
- For Crike's sake, don't get out a list of questions! This is a date, not an inquisition.
- A first - or fiftieth - date is not the time to discuss your ex from hell's bad habits. If your date asks, say something like

"he was a decent guy but we grew apart." If he is not a decent guy, you could mention he is no longer in your life.

- Most men don't appreciate gossip about your friends or co-workers.
- If you do talk about your job, keep it to the positive aspects and leave out the horror stories. This is sometimes difficult to accomplish.
- Don't brag about your job, either. You could inadvertently intimidate him or attract a fortune hunter.
- Your attention belongs to your date, so turn down your cell phone and don't text, sext, or surf the Net.
- Don't bring along anyone else with you. Chaperones are not necessary. It's 2012, not 1880.
- Even happy talk about your job can be a yawn-a-rama for your date.
- If you aren't attracted to him or know you could never be, stay courteous and non-committal. If he calls you after your date you can always use the old "my boyfriend's back" exit.
- Don't talk in detail about your family. When Mr. Wrong brought pictures of Mom and told me how wonderful she is, the already miserable date didn't get any better.
- It's easy to be a brilliant conversationalist. All you have to do is be an attentive listener.

- Fill an awkward silence by asking a question. It doesn't have to be anything profound and shouldn't be anything too personal or controversial. Is he a Chevy or Ford man? What was his kindergarten teacher like? If it sounds silly, perhaps you can both laugh and get the date back on track.
- Of course, you don't bring a first date home, no matter how strong your feelings for him or how long you've been alone. Sex on a first date almost guarantees there will be no second.
- If your date makes you uneasy, is rude, or isn't what he said he was, make a graceful exit.

If you would like to encourage him, rest your head on his shoulder, brush your hand lightly against his, gently tap his arm. You could also offer to read his palm while looking into his eyes, smiling. Slow, easy and gentle – feminine. You were born a flirt. We all were.

How can you tell if he likes you? Does he move in close to you? Does he touch your arm when he talks to you?

However, don't read too much into his actions. It takes time to develop a relationship so let your first date be an opportunity to get to know each other.

If you would like a second date, a simple "Thanks. I had a great time" will give him the all clear to ask you out again.

You took pains to look your best, so forget your appearance! My car's emergency box contains a hair brush, cologne, baby wipes, and hand cream for last minute touch-ups.

Little things mean a lot. Although a recent admirer is a year younger than my son - yes, you read that correctly - he still pursued a romance with me. No, it was just too weird for me, although it could work for anyone else, and I let the guy down gently. What attracted me to him? My lip gloss!!! You'd better believe that I now touch up my lipstick instead of letting it wear off during the day, and yes, I've picked up a few new tubes since my quasi romance. Thanks for the reminder - here's a little pink raspberry being splashed onto my (still kissable!) lips right now!!!

Not Even Spellcheck Would Help

A competitor in our quest for everlasting love wants to meet a "good looking well manured man". She has a good shot at finding what she says she is looking for because according to some all men are full of sh*t. Perhaps she should refine her search for a well "mannered" man. Good luck with that. ☹

Over a year ago, a blind date left me standing in the lobby of a local restaurant. My crime? I was "too fat to be seen with." (He was also chubby, but as an eighty pounds overweight man once told me, "A man can cover his extra twenty pounds by wearing a suit, but a woman can't hide.") I wish I could thank my date, because his honesty, no matter how it hurt me at the time, turned my life around.

First dates can be like job interviews: either weeding out the poor fits, or looking for things in common. So - never argue, never get too independent and stand out. Unless he speaks extreme opinions 180 degrees opposed to your way of thinking, and he is belligerent, smile and find common ground. If he's a total freak, smile and make a graceful exit. Crazy might be fun at first, but is wearing while you are living your lives together. You might end up married to a man who spends his spare time attempting to contact space travellers. Oh, no, wait - that was my guy!! And at the time it seemed perfectly normal!

If you wonder if he is The One, please keep in mind that a man in love defends his woman, no matter what. Even if you do something ridiculous, he does not criticize you. You and he are on the same team, He & You Against The World. A man who sees "the other side" of an argument with your mother or friend, or your work problems, is not loyal to you! When you love, you love, and you take up for your man, don't you? Do you deserve less from the man you love? Fair and impartial is for a judge and jury, not your lover. Rational and reasoning is not romantic! You of course extend the same loving courtesy toward him. If he has too many troubles, then bail on the relationship. Don't try to change him, don't criticize him, don't pick at him. Find someone who thinks as you do.

Another black flag is if he pays more attention to others than to you when you are out. This is so elementary that it sounds silly to mention it, but when a guy is besotted with you, he literally doesn't see anyone else. And "I see you all the time" as an excuse to leave you on your own at a family (his) get together doesn't cut it. If he wants to circulate, he should leave you home. Yes, yes, you are a grown woman, and you are perfectly capable of making your own small talk, but why would a man "abandon" you? It's happened to this gal, with two different men, one a fiancé (his Mommy broke that up), the other a husband (ditto about Mommy), and believe me, it's not going to happen with a third man. (And neither is Mommy meddling.) As they get a little older some women feel the Mommy problem is automatically solved (as Mommy has passed on), but it's not about Mommy, it's about a man not putting you and you first. One man I dated briefly was so nice, so kind, attractive, financially secure – and overly involved with his step-daughter and her toddler. He wanted to see me, but Christine needed him to babysit, Christine needed money, Christine's ex didn't pay child support, he changed more diapers than the baby's father. He was a better father to Christine than her natural dad, too. He was always there for her, and he always would be, and any woman who came into his life would have to understand that. Why didn't he date Christine? So what if she was just twenty-one to his fifty? . They weren't blood relatives. She was his life. There was no room for anyone else. He did buy me an expensive steak dinner and he did have red hair. I would have loved to have been courted by him.

One thing about the over forty man is that he sometimes wants the woman to take control of the relationship. He's been married once, or a few times, and he's used to the woman taking care of all the emotional aspects of a relationship. Many women enjoy this situation. I do not. It is not romantic.

26

Other Roads to Romance

A co-worker's sister tried an evening of speed-dating with an introductory offer of $46 but said a full membership cost a small fortune. You converse with ten different men in five minute "dates" and the next day you find out if there are any matches. When I visited the website to reserve my spot (one night, not a full membership!), I found out that women in my age group (46-59) would have to be put on a waiting list as all spots were filled. Returning men could re-up with no problem. So - even if there were enough cancellations to allow me to attend, men in my age group would be "spoiled" by the law of averages.

Men and women in the 22-32 had no waiting lists; men in every age group had no waiting lists, and women in every group above the age of 32 had too much competition! For the more confident, speed dating could work, but the possibility of eight rejections in one night is unthinkable for the shy. My 20 something co-worker decided to go for it and think of it as an experience. When she wears make-up she looks like Britney Spears, but she doesn't see it. She wants to wear a Barbie tiara to the speed date but admits she is thinking more of jeans and a t-shirt.

Weed dating was a new one on me, but I like the idea. Weed dating does not refer to "medicinal herbs" but good old fashioned farm work. According to what little (one article printed on several websites) I was able to find on the Internet, weed dating is sprouting up in rural areas of Idaho, Illinois, Ohio, Michigan, Wisconsin and Vermont. However, the only details I found involved Idaho. The ground rules involve each woman being assigned to a specific section of the garden after having been given a short and intense training in vegetable and fruit identification. Playing a farmer in the dell version of musical chairs, each man works in a bed for three minutes before going on to the next.

Since I could not find a weed dating venue in my area, I am considering starting on through meetup.com. (Or more likely, wait for someone else to do it.)

If you want to make new friends and expand your social horizons, check out www.meetup.com. There are nearly three million members and thousands of groups, for just about any interest - political, art, music, sports, dogs, at home moms, exercise, you name it – and the beauty of this is that your meetings are in person, not online! It's free to join an existing group, or you can start your own. You decide how far you are willing to drive. I signed up, with a 25 mile radius, and hopes of meeting like minded individuals, friends as well as The One.

According to Meetup's website, over 9,000 groups get together in local communities each day. Anyone can organize a local group or join one already meeting up face-to-face. It took me months to be able to attend a hike. If it wasn't a scheduling conflict (working two jobs leaves so little free time), it was hikes I knew I could never complete (nine miles of rugged terrain – three is my limit). A walk through a few acres of woods and perennials was my first experience. It will not be my last.

Parks in metropolitan areas often have walking/hiking and other activities including crafts. Check out adult education classes at your local community colleges, art centers or Y. At the very least you could make a new friend while learning a marketable or fun skill. I look forward to attending a stained glass and/or mosaic class.

Last fall I attended a Singles in Agriculture all day event after finding out we would tour a washboard factory, something that I had been wanting to do. We then cruised a few blocks down the street for an odyssey through the past via the five building county historical society. Next up, our group of eighteen or so women and two men (both attractive) ate lunch at a locally owned diner before forming a caravan to the Hocking Hills for a hike where my journey ended. I didn't have the heart for the square dance that evening. A nine to one ratio was too much for this single to even attempt to overcome. I look forward to further adventures with this group.

I recently (almost) met someone in Real Time, by chance, the best way, who could have been The One. On the way to the site of the former Athens Lunatic Asylum to take pictures of the post Civil War campus/ruins, I saw a man dumping out a raccoon (into a woods that looks to be private property). I stopped the car and rolled down my window to tell him I do the same thing almost every day. I didn't say that I use public parks because I didn't want to seem bossy. He said this was his eighth and if they didn't leave him alone he would start eating them. Ha, ha, ha. Wait until he's hitting sixty raccoons and ten 'possums. Committing such a furtive – and illegal -- act, he probably was too nervous and eager to peel and squeal his exit to spend the time to get to know me. Or, I've been reading too many novels starring an offbeat bounty hunter and her grandma.

☠🖱_____

Worse than WTF?

Beware: He makes house calls to provide massages to older lonely, divorced or widowed, women. He's young, very discreet and doesn't care what you look like. He will pamper you. Sounds like something a Craigslist Killer would post. ☹

Single's Night.

It was only 8:29 p.m. and I made a stop on the way home (I left the house after 7:00) so I guess it is obvious the big Single's Night didn't work out.

It was at a comfy, lived in, run-down bar, right off the highway.

Two young guys were escaping their fate as I walked in. They were literally beating feet leaving the bar and getting into their truck. It was a nice truck, which I pointed out. "Thanks." They didn't peel and squeal, but they also didn't waste a second in their getaway.

When I went in, three very bored women, one of them puffing on her ciggie, briefly looked me over (obviously I am no competition as they were much younger). My t-shirt sporting a huge sunflower and handkerchief miniskirt must not have fit in with the tight jean gals. I sat down. A middle aged thin guy wearing plaid pants standing by the bar didn't make eye contact with anyone. No one bothered to speak to me, so I got up and went home.

It was a very depressing place.

P.S. I looked my best and was in a pleasant mood. It just wasn't for me.

When I emailed the dating website, the moderator said, "Did you speak to anyone?" No, I didn't. Did I expect people to come to me? Don't I feel I need to reach out, too? When I am with others, I always speak to someone alone, but when I am alone I don't approach a group of people. It's not only intimidating, but it also seems a bit of intrusion on my part.

Not My Mr. Right, but Perhaps Yours. One guy who wanted to meet me was pictured wearing a much too tight t-shirt sitting at a flea market. He probably is very nice, but bargain hunting is something I share with friends and not a guy. Even then, this is an occasional pursuit, not a steady interest. From the picture he appears to be a seller, and that's not how I want to spend my week-ends. There are many lovely women who would love to share this activity, though. Oh, ok! He is extremely overweight.

WTF?

This "gentleman" is seeking lady who is ready for an ongoing ANR/ABF relationship. This is an acronym I refuse to google. It can't stand for anything healthy. ☹

One guy is open to a LTR with the right woman, or more specifically, the right pair of feet. He's not into pain or chains (????) but he wants to remove your shoes and kiss your feet, then give you a loving foot massage at the end of the work day. Age and race are not important to him. I had corresponded with a man with a foot fetish previously, and although it didn't shock me, I also had no interest. My feet are ugly! I walk! It's difficult enough keeping hands soft and smooth (and for several winter months each year, it is nearly impossible), and I am not going to worry about my feet being "attractive" enough for a romantic encounter.

This ad was from a dating (not explicit sex) site. He is upfront with what he wants, so please don't lie about your physical attributes. Can we even discuss this? He wants a large clitoris. Your age is unimportant, but he would like you to be a nice girl, yet sadistic. He also describes his methods of "self abuse" but again, it's just too much for us. I will tell you that he does "weird" things I have never heard of. He will be happy to send pix of his little friend, Red Baron, to nice girls. Again, the language of this particular keyboard Romeo has been cleaned up.

I thought about contacting this "gentleman" so that I could add him to this book, but even I have my limits.

His ad states he is already dating four "nice" ladies and is looking for a fifth. He wants a different woman, Monday through

Friday nights, and then two lucky ladies will be chosen from the five to spend Saturday and Sunday with him. He hastens to add that one is for Saturday, the other for Sunday, not two at a time. He would not anyone to think he is a jerk. He has a job and is fun-loving. At least he isn't married. I wonder if the ladies know about each other. What is the criteria for being chosen as one of the weekend women? Is Saturday or Sunday the plum date? Where does he get his stamina? Not just sexually, but where does he get the energy to go out every night of the week? When does he have time to do his laundry? Does he pay for dinner or do the women go dutch treat?

☠🖱_____

WTF?

A 52 year old charmer is seeking an "elderly" woman, aged 49 to 56. ☹

One man states he is looking for a second wife. This one I could not figure out - is he a bigamist or serial husband? He said you should be open minded, and he will give you all the love and sex and romance you could ever want, and that you deserve his kind attentions. He does require that you have a job. I wonder if his first wife will also shower you with love, sex, romance and attention. Do you each provide a home, and he takes turns visiting you the way Grandma gets passed around? Or does he have a place of his own? Menage a trois? No thanks.

Many men are looking for flings, and the woman they are targeting ("dreaming of" is too romantic a term for what these guys want) should not be overweight, or have any other "faults" that most women carry.

Why would a man state that he does not "beat the crap" out of the woman in his life, or cuss her or call her filthy names? Can't he come up with anything positive? I didn't respond, but do wonder about the women who did. And there are always women who do respond.

I really don't get this guy: Looking for a fun, attractive older woman to help with chores around the house. If you put him to work, he would like you to buy him a few drinks. Picture required.

It is not uncommon for men to advertise looking for a date to accompany them to concerts. Recently a man wants to take a "slender to average" sized woman aged 44 to 49 to see Bob Seger. You must provide a RECENT (his caps) picture to be considered. He seems nice enough, but this is his second (to my knowledge) ad, so I am wondering if any of us is up to his standards for physical beauty.

One man took me to see Tom Petty the last time he was in town. Tom was kickin', but I never heard from my date again.

Men looking for friends with benefits at least are upfront about not wanting to be bothered with a woman except for a quick hook-up. You are likely not that woman. (You certainly don't have to be.)

Many men are looking for flings, and the woman they are

targeting ("dreaming of" is too romantic a term for what these guys want) should not be overweight, or have any other "faults" that most women carry.

Why would a man state that he does not "beat the crap" out of the woman in his life, or cuss her or call her filthy names? Can't he come up with anything positive? I didn't respond, but do wonder about the women who did. And there are always women who do respond.

Kerry is seeking someone who doesn't have seven kids by seven different men – or even the same father, who didn't drop out of high school, doesn't have more animals than a zoo, isn't so fat she has to buy two airline tickets (if she could afford to fly) or isn't allowed on elevators , doesn't force her daughters to participate in pageants, doesn't have a deranged, demented, jealous, possessive ex who will slash his tires and firebomb his house, isn't a druggie, drunk or metalhead, doesn't dress like a tomboy, goth, or tramp, and finally, doesn't leave the g's off words ending in "ing." I'm not for him. I have too many pets, often drop the "g", and at times am something of a tomboy. Although not a goth, I recently attended a goth BBQ, which is exactly like any other cook-out, I'm too old to be a metalhead and I've never been tempted by a drug, prescription or street. Timothy must have a colorful romantic past to be able to come up with such a list.

It is not uncommon for men to advertise looking for a date

to accompany them to concerts. Recently a man wants to take a "slender to average" sized woman aged 44 to 49 to see Bob Seger. You must provide a RECENT (his caps) picture to be considered. He seems nice enough, but this is his second (to my knowledge) ad, so I am wondering if any of us is up to his standards for physical beauty.

One man took me to see Tom Petty the last time he was in town. Tom was kickin', but I never heard from my date again.

Men looking for friends with benefits at least are upfront about not wanting to be bothered with a woman except for a quick hook-up. You are likely not that woman. (You certainly don't have to be.)

Beware the upper income executive (or "exe" as he spells it - there is no cost or word limit so he could reasonably spell it out) man looking for a woman from the same side of the tracks. This man is "not a snob" but he posts regularly stating no trailer park gals for him. One would assume man with a high earning potential could spell and use proper grammar but this frequent browser is nearly illiterate. He prefers married women. Maybe I'll respond, arrange a meeting, and show up in a pick-up truck, wearing my NASCAR jacket - and reject HIM!

One guy posted a picture, not of himself, but of the cartoon character dad on The Family Guy with his shirt pulled up to reveal a "No Fat Chicks" t-shirt. How "whitty" (as some spell it)!! We can imagine how handsome, cultured and personable he is.

WTF?

Tall, highly educated, married man will whip a deserving young lady with his belt. Any reply must be respectful with details of your sexual history and marital status. Long term relationship possible, you lucky devil. ☹

A middle aged man really IS looking for his second (as in bigamous) wife: Non-smoker, non-drinker, professional "type", educated, gainfully employed, kind, fun, honest man, 6', well built, is keeping his current wife and find another woman to join the family. If you think you could fit in, send Don a message. Well, Donnie baby, I don't think I could fit in, so I will not be dropping you a line. Say hi to your wife.

WTF?

No experience necessary. He'll teach you how to drywall. He works naked, but you can wear a see through plastic poncho if that would make you more comfy. Orange juice provided. ☹

Local is good, right? Since geography had not been my friend I decided to give highest priority to guys living close by and not considering anything else. MISTAKE FOUR. Vernon wasn't coy. His first email included his expectations for a relationship, i.e., what is my favourite type of porn? I don't like pornography. As it turns out, Vernon's wife of over twenty years – you remember Harriet, don't you? – Harriet, the wife we never realized existed - doesn't, either. Vernon confided that "insect" porn is his favourite genre. Although he most likely didn't mean the mating habits of arthropods, termites, ticks, bedbugs, beetles, cockroaches, cooties, daddy longlegs, fleas, gnats, lice or other vermin, even that is preferable to movies about inbreeding or as the more highly educated would term it, Electral and/or Oedipal love. Since he says he has been in the closet for thirty years, why did he contact me?

One man, my age, was a retired teacher, living only a few miles away. Since I don't understand the concept of retirement, possibly because I might never be able to stop working and may not even want to, a retired man is not a good match for me. This man was in his mid fifties. If he was retired, what did he do all day? Did he volunteer at the hospital, read to the blind, walk shelter dogs? He made it quite clear that since he was retired, he would not be spending money on wining and dining any woman. If his retirement income weren't enough, why didn't he get a part-time job? This was something I wondered, but kept to myself. Cheap with finances, cheap with emotions has been my experience.

He wanted me to come to his house to meet him. I don't go to men's homes. He assured me that students frequently visited him, so I would be perfectly safe. It had nothing to do with safety. Being ever so cooperative, he then gave me his phone number. I was to call him. He didn't get it. Romance! The excitement of waiting for his call, planning our first date, dressing up and going out. What century am I living in? If I won't come over to his house, and I won't call him, there is no chance for a relationship. I am obviously very stubborn. He does not as he feels that romance is silly and a waste of time. He wants a woman in his life, and doesn't want to play games. However, since we do live close to each other, we can compromise: If I call him, he'll meet me at McDonald's – for coffee. How could any woman resist this Cassanova, you ask? Also, it must be noted that although he is retired, he is still in his fifties. I'll be working until I am seventy and am looking for a man similarly situated. I do not want to get up and go to work, leaving a man at home all day, regardless of his retirement or disability income. If he truly does not need to work for financial reasons, then he could spend his days volunteering. Oh, what a hard woman I am. But I am the daughter of a very hard working man and the widow of a very hard working man – wait, they are both dead. Perhaps I should lighten up a little. A man doesn't have to be a beast of burden, does he? But offering to buy me a cup of coffee at McDonald's?? That's our courtship?

Another local man found me equally uncooperative. We

emailed for the first time during heavy snowfall. He wanted us to meet immediately. Could we wait a day or two until the roads were clear? It's one thing driving on ice to go to work, but skating around on the highway at night is something else. He updated his profile, this time spelling things out: as a recently divorced man, he needed a live-in love ASAP to assist with the mortgage and to help support his seventeen year old daughter who would be going off to college within a year. He was good looking enough, if his picture were to be believed, and was professionally employed, so he was a catch for the right woman.

My name is Carol, but one half of a Mike and Carol Brady I'll never be. My kids are grown, and my dogs probably don't count.

When Timothy called me we ended up talking for an hour. We have everything in common! We reminisced about a local eccentric woman of our youth, complete with the fishing hat with hooks hanging off it, cruising the drive-ins, me finding excuses to stop at a drug store where the cute Catholic school boys (himself included) hung out. He smokes. I do not. End of story. His choice. He'll always smoke and he doesn't want to get involved with a woman who doesn't. P.S. He's seen my photo on several dating sites and thinks I'm attractive, and he's every bit the cute Catholic boy he ever was.

Not Even Spellcheck Would Help

Although this man is willing to accept a little extra weight, even more depending on how you carry it, his preference is "skinning." ☹

Men in Uniform

Well built, brave young men in firefighter uniforms, riding in Big Fire Trucks, carrying axes, running into burning buildings to rescue children, the elderly, puppies and kitties. Your town's Finest, shoes and holsters spit shined, walking the mean streets to ensure our safety. Sailors in their dress blues. Soldiers in camo fatigues. Military uniform and white sparkly gloves. Nothing beats a sharp dressed man in his military uniform. Neat, clean, fit, perfectly put together, strong, brave. Doctors in scrubs. UPS drivers look good, too, as do Pepsi deliverymen. Cowboy boots, chaps and Wranglers. Leather jackets and motorcycle helmets. (I personally don't want a biker, nice guys that they most probably are.)

If you meet any of these men through online dating, let us know which site so we can join, too.

Unfortunately I've never met an available one   No, the men in uniform that I attract sport the Elmer Fudd look: plaid jackets and hunting caps, minus the shotguns. Not a player in the bunch; these men are definitely looking to get married. Unfortunately, they left out a vital step in dating to mating: romance.

I have gone out on introductory dates with these men who merge in my memory as short guys who wear hunting caps, and I cannot remember even one name. Please do not think I am too "picky" or that I am stuck on myself because nothing could be further from the truth. Two of these interchangeable gentlemen (and they all were nice, as far as I could tell) took me to all you can eat breakfast buffets. One gave me the inside on a local murder: the wife's car was frequently parked in front of a single man's house. He also told me the name of the murderer. Even though I secretly agreed with him, I was not surprised when we were both proven wrong a few months later. Either he or the other guy who looked just like him (through my eyes) and took me to breakfast at the time place told me he built his house himself, and missed going to drive-ins (as in *Happy Days* episodes).

Most of us wouldn't wear plaid on a first date/meeting, but we of the fairer gender were raised on *Seventeen*, *Glamour* and *Cosmopolitan* and we know how to look our best. We might not always take the time to be alluring, but we know when to wear war paint and when to keep our powder dry.

How many men have you ever known to read *GQ*? Would you trust a guy who did?

Perhaps the hunting cap worn through dinner is meant to "hide" a receding hairline. How long will a man keep that secret? Will he continue wearing it on your honeymoon? You and your groom in a hot tub, a hunting cap and only a hunting cap the only item of clothing... Or consummating your marriage - with hunting cap firmly in place...

Elmer Fudd #1 didn't accept any of my lame excuses. He took me out, once, and then kept calling me.

Disinterested female (me): I'm not much of a housekeeper.

Interested male: That's ok because I don't like that kind of woman. I want someone independent, like you.

Over a breakfast buffet, one of the hunting cap guys (I can't remember which one) told me about his friend's daughter. She is very attractive, and he loves it whenever she is around, because she's so much fun. It was incredibly and uncharacteristically easy for me to say, "Have you ever thought about asking her out?" In my old life I was jealous and insecure, but now I am merely insecure, because I've learned that there are few men who worth green-eyed emotion. He smiled and replied, "She's a Jaguar, and I'm just a Volkswagen, and I know when I am out of my league. So I date VWs." Excuse me? I'm a sleek, red, classic five on the floor Dodge Daytona with silver ground effects, not a Volkswagen bug!! And you, Dear Reader, are at least a Mustang, too! There would never have been a second date, anyway, but did he really have to compare me to what he views as a cheap car? (I don't consider any means of transportation "cheap.")

No, he didn't offend me, because his opinion was not important to me. First dates should be magic, and I've had two of these - one man is in his grave, but I have his children and grandchildren and the other is My Count Vronsky and I have nothing of him - in my life, and now I'm looking for the third. I'll take nothing less.

After several months of romancing a girl on indefinite vacation at The Cross-Bar Hotel, Elmer Fudd #2 received a letter from the warden's office suggesting he stop sending money. It appeared that Ms. Right, Incarcerated, was encouraging the attentions (as well as checks and money orders) of several men. And you thought only women were so lonely that they had "pen pals"!

They don't wear red suits trimmed in white fur, but they may as well. Men come in waves, and one group that should have stayed at sea consisted of men who looked like Santa Claus. Oh, how I wish this were an exaggeration, but it's not. I don't want to date Santa Claus, or even a man who merely bears a strong resemblance to the beloved old guy.

Gray hair - or no hair - is fine. Long gray hair accompanied by an equally lackluster beard is not. It does not remind one of the Summer of Love. It instead screams, "old! my great-grandfather! Abraham Lincoln!"

Long, scraggly gray hair and beards is not an attractive look and neither is a rotund belly covered by a tight t-shirt stretched to an inch of its life. The benefit of being contacted by these men is that you can bet I'm keeping up with Clairol treatments, even if I am my own DIY hairdresser. For some reason, many of these men listed hobbies as going to flea markets. One's main picture was of him sitting by a table laden with "treasures." (I already have enough junk for three houses.) Accompanying a man to an occasional auction is one thing. Sitting at a flea market on my day off is another. Come to think of it, scratch the "occasional auction." I'd really rather be hiking. Or propped up in bed reading and drinking hot chocolate. Or ...

And these guys (paunch included) seem to gravitate toward me. One man started talking marriage ten minutes after I joined a free online dating service. That night I had a nightmare. I'm single, yes; romantic, yes; relationship friendly, yes. Desperate, no. Oh, and let's not kid ourselves. I'm nothing special. These men are "romancing" every woman within whatever parameters they set.

You may disagree, but guys with online pages with pictures and bios do not interest me. Several have suggested I check out their websites and get back with them if I see anything I like. What ever happened to pleasant conversation, flirting, dating?

If you wonder if he is The One, please keep in mind that a man in love defends his woman, no matter what. Even if you do something ridiculous, he does not criticize you. You and he are on the same team, He & You Against The World. A man who sees the other side of an argument with your mother or friend, or your work problems, is not loyal to you! When you love, you love, and you take up for your man, don't you? Do you deserve less from the man you love? Fair and impartial is for a judge and jury, not your lover. Rational and reasoning is not romantic! You of course extend the same loving courtesy toward him. If he has too many troubles, then bail on the relationship. Don't try to change him, don't criticize him, don't pick at him. Find someone who thinks as you do.

On your date, wear lightly scented, feminine cologne and apply make-up with a gentle touch. It's very tempting to go all out but it will come off more whole hog or desperation than flattering, to either him or you.

If you were left with a settlement or insurance money, keep this info to yourself. To men who ask how much life insurance a husband had, the answer is "he worked very hard for every dollar he made and he did the best he could." I personally also make it clear that I intend to continue working, regardless of any change in my marital status. I am contributing to my own Social Security fund and not depending on anyone else.

We can learn for this woman, if we so chose. She was widowed several years ago and has had several boyfriends. The last guy talked her into quitting her job and becoming a business partner in a get rich quick scheme. Partner is not quite accurate as she fronted 100% of the money and he contributed the brains of the operation. Since she did all the actual work, while he did all the actual thinking (with a bottle of Jack in his hands), she had to quit her paying job.

After things went sour, they broke up, and she lost everything, including the home that was paid off by her husband's life insurance.

She is now working full-time and works a part-time job on both Saturday and Sunday and she still doesn't know if she can keep her head above water.

When he called her, told her he loved her and wanted her back, she told him she had never stopped loving him and she believes everything will work out.

Inspiring romance. Remember the old perfume commercial: want him to be more of a man? Try being a woman. It's a slogan that works.

Romantic gestures that will lure him closer include feminine hair, soft cologne, bright smiles, flattering clothing, your soft voice ...in every way be a girl whatever your age, weight, height. Listening to him without interrupting or criticizing or explaining what he should do/really means is something that he craves. Let him come home to you, the one person in this world who is always on his side, always sees his point of view. If he's a total idiot, or a chronic liar, or other loser, you aren't going to be with him anyway, so it's safe to let him be himself around you. He can relax when he's with you because he knows you understand him, and in spite of knowing him inside and out, you approve of him.

Some magazine articles suggest baking heart shaped cupcakes for anniversaries or Valentine's Day and giving him a bath, shampoo and massage at the end of the day, but until he is madly, insanely in love with you, don't go out of your way to show your love as it will only scare him away. He's The Big Game Hunter as you recall. Even some married men don't care for such displays of affection from their wives. Don't ask me why!! But in most cases, being elusive wins a man's heart.

Men on my radar screen: There is a Rob Thomas lookalike working at metropolitan library. I hadn't seen him in awhile, which is too bad, because the last time he checked me out he said, "Thanks, Baby." So when I returned my books today I said, "You look so much like Rob Thomas." He smiled his crooked grin. I said, "People probably tell you that all the time" to which he replied, "No, no one ever says that."

Too bad he's much too young for me. And when I think someone is too young, that means he's at least twenty years younger.

But I think he enjoyed the compliment.

If you are dating a much younger man and someone makes a catty remark, deflect by replying sweetly, "You could get a young guy if you wanted." This can be a true statement or sarcasm to someone who is merely jealous of your relationship. For a true witch, the response could be, "Not every woman can land a younger man." Since your dating life, or the age of any suitor, is not anyone else's business, ignore the comments and never let anyone else sabotage your relationship or your confidence to attract and keep a man. Remember the old saying, "The dogs bark, but the caravan moves on."

Dating Married Men, by me, a hypocrite who was once in love with My Count Vronsky.

This one's easy: Don't. Build your self-esteem to the point that you aren't begging for crumbs from someone else's table. Another don't: Don't steal another woman's husband. Love is not a competition and only under the most extreme circumstances could it ever be anything but hostile to behave in such a manner. She doesn't deserve it, he's not worth it, and you are above it. That said, most women at one point or another in life, become entangled in such a triangle. Enjoy it, if you insist, but keep your powder dry. This means no chasing after him, no waiting around for him, no pining away for a life that most likely will never be.

That said, you might as well do it right.

Protect yourself, respect yourself.

Some women try to push men into relationships, but a personal favorite of mine is, "Give 'em enough rope to hang..." Don't call, don't beg, don't plead, don't ask – for anything. Live your own life and enjoy your romance.

Have you ever been the other woman? If you have, one thing you've learned (other than that you get the short end of the stick and no matter what's going on his marriage, he's not likely to leave her for you) is that if a woman insists on her husband kissing her butt, he will look around so that he can kiss a more delicious part of another woman.

Getting dumped (while still healing from previous trauma). Yes, it hurts, and sometimes you feel like a fool, but at the very least, you gave love a try. Married guys are a recipe for disaster and no matter what puppy dog eyes the cheater gives you, run, don't walk, away. My Count Vronsky was married, and intends to stay married forever. Church. Responsibilities. Kids. His soulful eyes and self-deprecating smile - how I could I ever resist? I didn't. He came and went, running away when he felt we were getting too close, coming back when things got too difficult at home. Oh, I could never tell him my real feelings. "I love you" would have been the death knell for the "relationship."

☠🖱_____

WTF?

Tommy Lee seeks Pamela Anderson. Mention boats in your message so he knows you are his one and only.   ☹

Insecurity. If you are worried about holding on to him while you are dating, don't. Don't worry and don't date him. If he makes you insecure, he's not for you. If you are ever tempted to check his private email account, his phone log, or any other personal effects, baby, you are on the wrong track. If you are this jealous, either he is feeding your insecurity and he is guilty of not loving you enough, or you need to build your self esteem and live your own life.

How good does spying make you feel? Even if you find you are wrong, do you feel any better? How about if you are right about him? We've all been entangled with men, perhaps even one-sidedly, who find someone else more interesting, and to make things even worse, the women are never as attractive, friendly, or intelligent as we are!

No stalking! You know what that means. No driving past his house, no calling just to hear his voice on his answering machine message, no love letters – anonymous or not, no cute cards, no little presents. Definitely never give or loan any man money.

Oh, and dare we say it? Hold off on the hearts and flowers tattoo with his name on your derriere until at least your first wedding anniversary.

Need help with men? Follow the guidelines your mother or grandmother nagged you about. "Why buy the cow when you can get the milk for free?" was the most annoying piece of advice I've ever heard, but it's probably as true today as it ever was.

I memorized the tips my mother gave me. They work. And, I never play by any rules. I'm not prey and men aren't Big Game Hunters. I hate games, always have. My ideal man also doesn't want to play games or be manipulated. And, he'll be smart enough to see through the attempts of manipulation. In my estimation, a woman who resorts to tricks is weak and or desperate.

The closest I ever got to playing the game was when My Count Vronsky called and wanted to meet me at 6:00. Normally I fly out the door when he calls, but not this time. "John John needs his medicine at 6:00." "I thought you might be able to give it to him a little early." I stood my ground, and he was not upset with me. "He has to have his meds at 12 hour intervals or he could die." So, even though My Count Vronsky had his Prior Commitment waiting for him to come home from work, he met me after 6:00 so that I could take care of my dog. And he was glad to see me!

Meanwhile, I'm alone, except for the men I ignore and don't want. I average one call a week from guys like this, and sometimes they come in clusters, occasionally one phone call after another.

Me, as Disinterested female: I'm not much of a housekeeper.

Interested male: That's ok because I don't like that kind of woman. I want someone independent, like you.

Looking back, I should have given this guy a chance. Unfortunately, he was short and wore a plaid hunting jacket and cap.

But as I often asked my mother, if men want what they can't have and if you have to play hard to get, what happens after you're married? They know they have you, then. She never answered.

Another theory that is making its rounds these days is criticizing the person you are interested in so that he knows you are good enough for him. Do you like being criticized? Are you critical of people you care about? Perhaps it would work, but some of us are women of heart and soul.

Here are dating tips for women who don't want to play by any rules, learned through trial and error. Perhaps you want "The One" not "The Prize."

You probably already realize this, but you have to allow yourself to be vulnerable, open to life's possibilities. Not closed.

It can be scary to put yourself out there, but it's necessary. Shyness is an appealing quality and no one suggests you become an aggressive man chaser, but let your interest in life show. Loving life is so attractive, so appealing.

One mistake, according to reliable sources (guess which gender!), some women make is wearing too much jewelry. Some men feel it is aging, others, distracting. Also, if you have rings on your fingers, how is Mr. Right or Mr. Right Now or even Mr. Close Enough to know you're available? Make it easy! Keep your left hand, at least, ring free.

Also, if a man lives thousands of miles away and you aren't willing or able to relocate, you'll stay single. Although many of us say we want a boyfriend, we do encourage impossible relationships. This way - no muss, no fuss, just romance!!

I practiced for a week after reading a book describing an alluring smile. When setting your bait, don't grin like an idiot, and certainly don't stand around with a bored look on your face, but instead have an anticipatory smile. This means have a pleasant look on your face as if you are ready to break into a warm, inviting smile at the approach of Mr. Right.

This is harder than you might think. My anticipatory smile involves upturned lips and raised eyebrows (somewhat like a dog listening for the sound of an electric can opener).

This is a tip for all your NASCAR babes. Place the decal of your favorite racer on the driver's side of your vehicle and leave the passenger's side clear. #24 is my favorite by a Daytona lap, but when I considered putting my second favorite #22 on the right side, I realized my car would look like it belonged to a couple, not a single woman. Who knows who might see me driving up and down the highway? What if Mr. Right stops to fill 'er up the same time I do, but he assumes I am married?

While you certainly should not gaze until his eyes (he'll assume you are planning your wedding), you also should not watch every other man that walks by, no matter how cute the physique.

Ask questions to show your interest. If you keep up on current events, at least superficially - it seems no one has time for anything in depth these days - you will have something to talk about.

Sports is always an easy, interesting conversation. I don't follow football, which is a sin when you live in Ohio (how about them Buckeyes?), but I do take a gander at the newspaper to see if they've won or lost their last game.

You should keep your "Oprah" topics for your female friends. Your interest in astrology, magik and other subjects of the occult probably will not dazzle a heterosexual man. How your sign relates to his, regardless of how true your observations might be, is another romance blocker, if not actual killer. You may of course look up your compatibility and research his sun sign characteristics. Just keep it to yourself!

What if he asks if you are interested in marriage (and you are)? Truthfully, you are looking for a nice guy and will see where it leads. Please don't give the impression that you are desperately lonely, financially ruined, or in any other way needy.

There are very few white knights these days and men who portray themselves that way perhaps should watched carefully.

Lying in bed a few nights ago, I heard Lionel Richie's "Hello" play over and over and over in my head. Of course I took that as a sign that someone (just didn't know who) was thinking about me. In the past, I've found out that this has actually happened, sometimes by the person I was thinking and others by a complete wild card.

We are going to end this chapter about dating and romance the same way we started: Do not chase men. Do not call them, do not write them, do not pay attention to them. Do not pretend to be friends when you are secretly in love with them. Look your best, keep busy, and let The Hunter capture your heart.

Perhaps an embittered aunt cautioned you that men "are only after one thing." She might have been right! However, the "thing" some of the men are after is money, not your pure heart or juicy body.

Handyman needs help. He will be working at the other end of town so he hopes Ms. Right will fix him a light lunch, let him use her shower, and she can take it out in trade.

Cheap, cheap! He is looking for a companion. You two could go to dinner, go fishing, take walks, stay in and watch movies. He doesn't drink or drug but does smoke. Pay your own way.

Good looking SWM, professional. Clean-cut, 6'1', 195 pounds, blue eyes, friendly smile. His interests include movies, reading, politics, and the environment. While he is affectionate, he is not interested in sex. Ever. He is 32 years old.

Now accepting applications for the following position: Fulltime girlfriend. Relevant requirements: Must have a job, your own transportation, high school diploma, and a place to stay. Pay is based on experience. Applicants with the following interest should apply: In addition to music applicants must also like comedies, beer, camping, fishing, bonfires, demolition derbies, bowling, and gaming. Applications will be held on file for 90 days, or until position is filled. No rehires.

This guy looks like an ex-con or addict. Long messy hair, skinny. However, he is single and looking for a sweet girl for a LTR. He's non-materialistic, low maintenance and likes the outdoors. Non-smoker, non drinker; keeps active. Password: guitar. Oh, please be younger (he's 48). Looking and acting like Rianna will put you at the top of the list.

☠🖱_____

WTF?

Although he's not gay or bi, he is curious and extremely interested in exploring with the right person(s). ☹

27

I Couldn't Resist

After reading an ad of a 46 year old man stating "I'm going through a rough time, and need the touch of a good woman" I responded simply: "I would contact you but you would probably tell me I'm too fat and/or too old."

Unfortunately, my "re:" line copied from his original stuck, making it appear that I, too, am 46. You've probably figured out that I am not 46 and haven't been for some time. I didn't bother correcting the title because I didn't expect anyone to reply.

Ding, dong! Was I ever wrong!

- Interested in making cash? Webcam jobs available.
- Several men sent emails with pictures (fully clothed, thank God) and no message.
- Promise_to_make_you_all_wet@___.com emailed me to tell me that I am not too old or fat for anyone. [I'll pass.]
- Two men said that they were sure I look great.
- A "military man" is busy but my words sound so sweet that he can't wait to hear from me.

- Another man told me I am beautiful inside and out, and no one is ever too fat or too old.
- "46 is not too old. Too fat, maybe, maybe not."
- How old? How fat? He has "taken down a few hogs." That is a lil joke, he hastens to add. Although he is HWP, he likes BBW.
- Would I be interested in a 50 year old corporate pilot?
- Grouchy old man needs cheering up. He likes older, heavy ladies and he can prove it.
- Wazz up? He's down with anything different and new.
- "I like fat women."

28

Faits Divers

(Translation from Francais to English - "Back Pages")

Each last potential beau becomes the last attempt. Until the next.

Keep in mind that it is best to take a man at his word. If he isn't looking for anything serious, don't think you will broadside him with your beauty and charm. If he has a type and you don't fit his criteria, he might never truly love you, even if he marries you. You might be the most gorgeous woman on earth, but if he wants someone anorexic, and you aren't, you will never be good enough for him. If you look like a model and he prefers an earth mother, the only way you will ever capture his heart would be to let nature take its course and put on some weight. Changing yourself for a man doesn't work, though, does it? If you aren't you, he can't fall in love with you.

I've refused several men who have asked me to meet them for "coffee." Why? Do you ever think that any man that cheap with his money would also be cheap with his emotions? Or, to be more practical, do you want to be involved with a cheapskate? One guy told me he was tired of paying for dates. If a woman isn't worth half a pizza or coffee plus dessert, how important or interesting can she be to him?

This has absolutely nothing to do with dating, but I thought it was funny. Miriam ran a successful sideline personal shopping business. "Personal shopping" is the perfect description for supplying customers with women's shoes, lingerie, adult diapers & bottles. Most are married who believe their wives are unaware of their little hobbies. When one of her best customers, an Ernest Bourgnine look-a-like, wanted her to find people that would let him model the lingerie, she gently refused. He persisted, requesting her to pimp him out; she told him no one would want to see him in a thong, for any amount of money, and closed down her service.

Ain't life grande?

The scent of grapefruit makes women appear younger to men. That's all well and good, but why aren't there studies conducted that give men hints how to be more attractive to women???!!! Here's a freebie for all the would be beaus: As a particularly distinguished (and irritating) man walked by, I thought, "If he smeared himself with chocolate, or even wore *eu de chocolat*, maybe someone could stand him."

If you have the money for a full treatment at an exclusive spa, it might be worth it. I don't so I set up my own.

A Dollar Tree Dolly's Version of a Spa

Bubble bath, oatmeal bath salts, bath oil beads or body shampoo – take your pick and dissolve it in your tub. Fill with water as hot as you dare, slip in with a non-alcoholic beverage and book or magazine. Relax and let the mood soothe you.

Use a facial scrub, then shampoo and condition hair.

Body scrubs whether from dollar stores or high end department stores are especially effective on neglected feet.

Wrap yourself in an oversized towel, grab a magazine, turn off your phone and turn on the tv, the more superficial the program the better. Slather on hand cream, top with moisture gloves, go to bed a little early, count your blessings and celebrate yourself and all that you have contributed to life.

Beautiful, Smooth Hands

If you complete the entire routine every week or two, your hands will need only easy daily maintenance.

Do you have any brown jersey gloves? Although "moisture gloves" are thinner they are harder to find. Brown gloves are generally available for anything between two pair for $1 to $1.18 for one pair. They are considered men's work gloves, they are ugly, they are absorbent, they are soft, they are sturdy, and they are an excellent value. If you have a crazy dog like my Eddie who tracks them down and greets you at the door by tossing them into the air, then running outside and burying them, you will appreciate their low price. If you are able to hold on to them, you will like their quality and durability. My mother used to go to bed (after my dad died) wearing white gloves, but they are hard to find, and expensive. At one time she would haunt thrift stores, which was indeed desperation for her as she was raised on second hand clothes, looking for gloves. She was probably too feminine to even realize men's products existed, let alone they are often an excellent bargain for women.

One a week if necessary, less frequently if not, use facial scrub to remove dry skin from your hands; rub in baby oil, let soak in, then slather, liberally, with a good quality hand cream. Udderly Smooth is inexpensive but lives up to its name. Pull on gloves and leave overnight or while doing gardening, walking, reading, anything that does not involve water. You can top with latex gloves if you need to wash dishes or clean house, but it tends to overheat and irritate my hands.

For years, I drove past a tavern whose logo was a headless woman. You don't want to be a woman who talks too much to the annoyance of the men in your life. That said, the type of men who hid in that type of bar probably deserved a sound scolding. Quick, now! Of those of all who have been married, what did we learn? "Kissin' don't last, cookery do?" Perhaps that was true for our great-grandparents. But what did we really learn? Yes! You got it! You cannot win an argument!!! A happy relationship consists of two people whose lives blend together, seamlessly. No arguing, no tantrums, no trying. If you have to work at a marriage, where's the fun? You have to work at work!

So if you get involved with a man, and problems pop up, and you go round and round and round about them, think about taking a walk. Permanently.

When a man treats you badly, "Sir, you are no gentleman!" said in your best Scarlett O'Hara works wonders. Whether you hail from Anchorage, or Albuquerque, or Albany, playing the part of a stricken southern belle just might put the cad in his place. Speaking of cads: In my opinion the "honorable Mr. Wilkes" was a true cad as compared with the honest red-blooded Cap'n Butler. Unfortunately, my tastes have always run to the Ashley Wilkes of this world. Even knowing this, nothing ever changes for me. Hey! That's Old Thinking and we are Going Forward without a Net. Now we will say, "In the past the Ashley Wilkes of this world have attracted me, but I am going to widen my horizons."

Go home, take a long hot bath, give yourself a pedicure and look forward to tomorrow, another day.

If you have gone a bit too far, too soon, you can salvage a bit of your reputation (with "him"! who cares about anyone else's opinion?) by wearing a silk flower in your hair, lacy or ruffled clothing, and hitting the delete key on any crude, rude, vulgar or nasty language. Speak more softly. Bat your eyes if you know how. This romantic approach will also draw a man into your orbit, painlessly. Well manicured nails never hurt, either.

Awhile back, I was called to a wedding in southern Ohio. This is from my blog: It's been awhile since my only other trek to Burr Oak, and this trip was ever so much more enjoyable than the other.

A boyfriend and I went on a road rally which ended up in a July barbecue/swim at a relative's cabin - HIS relative, not mine. We don't have second homes.

At that time with no fashion sense and being too "stupid" to wear a swimsuit to cover my "flaws" I had purchased a two piece blue and white checked design. At that time blue was my favorite color, and I loved the suit. It was cute. It was, however, not alluring or anything that is a must today, and apparently then. I just didn't get with the program.

Upon seeing me, the boyfriend exclaimed, "We're going to have to put you on a diet!" (I would have weighed less than 120 pounds.) You (or he) might not believe this, but he himself was no Brad Pitt (or Robert Redford). He could have been described as "chubby" but I would never have put him down that way.

It's funny now, but then I burst into tears. I can't remember what the reaction of the other rally club members was, or even if there was one.

In the intervening years, I've come to notice that no matter where I go, there are never super models in attendance and that no man would ever be mistaken for a movie star. Well, there was a guy who worked at Kroger had a slight Johnny Depp vibe, and even he didn't seem to be stuck on himself.

Mr. Boyfriend (aged 21) was ultra conservative, cautious, cheap (with everyone else but not himself), and owned two suits that his mother had picked out for him: one light blue iridescent and a similar light green one. He seldom wore the green, though. I didn't notice it then, but even with his long out of date Buddy Holly glasses and serious demeanor, he must have looked like a pimp when he dressed up. He had a Dodge Dart for everyday driving, and a Barricuda for the week-ends. His mother, a relatively young widow (the one thing we ended up having in common) uncharacteristically drove a purple Challenger. If the Ghost of the Past had shown up today, my Hyundai might have played chicken with Mr. Boyfriend.

He told me that after we got married he would like me to sew my own clothes like his mother, manage finances like his mother, and most importantly, cut up his oranges in segments for his lunch. I don't think to this day I have ever cut up anyone's oranges. My kids learned to peel them at a young age.

I almost forgot! While everyone was in the lake, the boyfriend came by and "playfully" pulled me under, then swam away. Yes, I was terrified, and yes, I nearly drowned. Two attempts at swim classes to erase my fear were unsuccessful. However, I enjoy my aging above ground pool. Walking in water is an excellent work-out and a great way to spend a summer day. I just don't let water anywhere near my face.

Looking back, the only positive thing I can say for the guy is that he had red hair.

Although "I Know You're Out There Somewhere" is one of my all time favorite songs, it doesn't remind me of Mr. Boyfriend, or anyone else.

This trip to Burr Oak was a fun drive down, a wonderful gig with friendly people, a tasty meal of roasted herbed new potatoes and beef stroganoff, and back roads all the way home. I even got to drive through Shawnee!

Today's "lesson": Don't let jerks (of either gender) get you down.

Even though I hadn't thought about him for a long time, every word about Mr. Boyfriend is true. I hope it made you laugh!

If you are nervous about meeting a guy, relax. Friend Ruth had occasion to meet her teen-age boyfriend after years of marriage and child rearing. "I look old! He'll be so disappointed!" Her daughter drove her to Chicago to meet Bernie, and guess who was disappointed? It sure wasn't Bernie! All through dinner, he couldn't keep his hands off Ruth. "It was awful! He wore a brown suit!" When Bernie tried to kiss Ruth, repeatedly, he ended up playing dodge 'em, because Ruth wanted no part of him. The next time you are frightened of rejection, remember Ruth.

Lukewarm Lovers. The number one qualification is enthusiasm! If he isn't thrilled to have you as his girlfriend, move on!

This is from Patty, an Internet friend: I meant to tell you before about my sister's experience with one of the pay match making sites. We filled out the questions together, which took several days, because she put so much thought into each one (she wanted the right match). Finally we are done, and it says ....NO MATCH. Then one night this man calls and asks for Linda. She says you have the wrong number. He calls back a few minutes later -- same thing -- says he has Gretchen Wilson tickets, and wants to take Linda, but must not have the right number. They start talking and he calls her every night for two weeks. They have a lot in common. He sounds great, and they agree to meet at a Chinese restaurant. When she gets there, he is standing outside, about two feet tall, with a cowboy hat on, and a Yosemite Sam mustache. It was love at first sight on his part, not so much on hers. She has had two more such experiences, so she is giving up. I just think they are not good enough men that deserve you two wonderful women, but I will still keep my fingers crossed.

Thanks, Patty. I'm not giving up and neither should you, Dear Reader.